Public Natures

Public Natures

Evolutionary Infrastructures

Weiss/Manfredi

Princeton Architectural Press, New York

Published by
Princeton Architectural Press
37 East Seventh Street
New York, New York 10003

Visit our website at www.papress.com

Publication of this book has been supported
by a grant from the School of Design at the
University of Pennsylvania.

Editorial Content: Allison Wicks
and Justin Fowler
PAP Editor: Meredith Baber
Designer: Project Projects

Special thanks to:
Sara Bader, Nicola Bednarek Brower,
Janet Behning, Erin Cain, Megan Carey,
Carina Cha, Andrea Chlad, Tom Cho,
Barbara Darko, Benjamin English,
Russell Fernandez, Jan Cigliano Hartman,
Jan Haux, Mia Johnson, Diane Levinson,
Jennifer Lippert, Katharine Myers,
Jaime Nelson, Rob Shaeffer, Sara Stemen,
Marielle Suba, Kaymar Thomas,
Paul Wagner, Joseph Weston, and
Janet Wong of Princeton Architectural Press
—Kevin C. Lippert, publisher

Public natures : evolutionary infrastructures /
Weiss/Manfredi. -- First edition.
      pages cm
   ISBN 978-1-61689-377-4 (hardback)
   1. Weiss/Manfredi Architects. 2. Space
(Architecture) 3. Urban transportation. I.
Manfredi, Michael A., 1953- II. Weiss, Marion,
1957-
   NA737.W398A4 2015
   711'.6--dc23
                 2014044331

Foreword

Barry Bergdoll

Surveying a decade of design work under the title *Public Natures*, Marion Weiss and Michael A. Manfredi have gathered a portfolio of their firm's work that blurs divisions between nature and building that craft the public realm. In doing so, they have opened the issue up to others, first to the profession, and now to readers, inviting other voices into their exploration of the stakes of design practice in a century when the public and natural realms are continually eroded. It is the realization that social, natural, and urban infrastructures are deeply intertwined and achieve potential through architectural and landscape thinking that makes this body of work more than a collection of exemplary designs, honed by the conditions of site and commission. Rather, each project is a catalyst both for local urban transformation and for a broader discussion about "public" and "nature" in a period when globalized urbanization, climate change, and planetary connectivity—with its paradoxical effects of social isolation—are all intertwined challenges. Many practices today focus on one of these; in the work of Weiss/Manfredi, multiple challenges are considered as inseparable conditions of intervention into the public realm.

It seems poignant that the office's rapid maturation as a leading force in reflecting—through form-making—on the vital stakes of placemaking in the twenty-first century started in 2001, the year of its selection in Seattle's Olympic Sculpture Park design competition. One can scarcely imagine a less propitious moment, as the terrorist attacks of 9/11 on key landmarks of American economic, political, and urban infrastructure ushered in a period that seemed to fulfill millenarian anxieties. While scholars dispute the direct connection, our new millennium began in 2001 with every bit as much anxiety as the "white mantle of churches"—that flurry of invention and creativity that spawned the continent-wide Romanesque style in the wake of the world's surviving the year 1000. Even if in retrospect the Y2K digital neurosis is largely forgotten, there is no doubt that 9/11 and the wars that followed, as well as the failure of trusted infrastructure during Hurricane Katrina in New Orleans and Superstorm Sandy in New York, ushered in what many feel is a world of a heightened sense of fragility. Resiliency is the challenge of the moment, as we think to build not for ephemeral effect but rather for sustainable evolution in the face of climate change, social insecurity, and the new relations that have been ushered in by the digital revolution. Yet the most remarkable development of the early twenty-first century is the ability of the design professions to rise to the daunting challenges that make headlines.

If "infrastructure" has become the byword of so many practices that blur the boundaries between architectural and landscape practice, it is because it encapsulates the challenges of scale and complexity that are the preconditions of meaningful public design work today. It is not surprising, therefore, that this word recurs at every scale of Weiss/Manfredi's reflection on their own work, from the descriptions of individual projects, to the categories established in this retrospective of a decade and a half of practice, to the titles of books done both within the firm and in their active teaching practice. What demarcates this diverse body of work from other forms of architecture are the common sensibilities, commitments, and thought processes that unite the architecture of the landscape in projects from Brooklyn to Seattle to Korea, with the innovative interior landscapes of buildings that restore and extend human colloquy in university and corporate research settings. Here one can see continuities between the firm's seminal Olympic Sculpture Park, highlighted in the Museum of Modern Art's 2005 Groundswell exhibition as heralding a new centrality of landscape thinking to urban architecture, and more recently completed projects such as the Diana Center at Barnard College and the Krishna P. Singh Center for Nanotechnology at the University of Pennsylvania. In all three projects, a zigzag visual path orders complex sectional thinking, a connection between disparate spaces and social settings; it serves equally as a device to resolve a host of complicated programmatic needs on a confined site. As in the tradition of the eighteenth-century English Picturesque approach to landscape design, the path of the eye and that of the foot are productively dissociated. But the comparison ends there; the aim is no longer the experience of the sole stroller to achieve individual stimulation and enlightenment, but to craft a new engagement of individuals with the collective and of the twin natures, humankind and natural realm, that vie with each other in cities and regions.

Weiss/Manfredi is interested in negotiating the divide between individual and communal work, between solitude for contemplation and the sense of belonging to a community, an interest that is achieved in a consummate way, for instance, in the Diana Center, a building that negotiates between spaces of intimacy and the interplay in a diagonal section of discrete spaces viewed one from another. These connections create for the teachers and students—for whom this building is a focal point of four years living in a community—a sense of their own work and activities as part of a larger social group within this intimate and compact college campus, which is divided by just a metal grill and greenery from the bustle of New York on the adjacent axis of Broadway. And perhaps most suggestively, the undergraduate studios of the Columbia/Barnard joint architecture program are housed here, in which architecture is taught as the crafting of a public realm in dialogue with the rest of the community. Weiss/Manfredi has recognized how vital this is for the most advanced scientific research of our time, bringing, for instance, the exploration of new nanotechnologies into productive internal encounters, but equally into the quotidian of the Philadelphia streetscape, as at the Krishna P. Singh Center at the University of Pennsylvania. It is as though the dynamic interweaving of activities and experiences through the existing infrastructure of the Seattle coastline in the Olympic Sculpture Park has here, at Penn, been internalized in a building set between a busy thoroughfare and the paths of a college campus, picking up the movement of one and the excitement of the other to create a zone that is at once of the city and apart from it. This seemingly irreconcilable dialogue between individual and communal, which is the very basis of successful communities, is a challenge that has been with architecture for centuries. Think of the emergence of the public library, in which architects designed spaces for reading alone in large communal settings—the very nature of which is changing radically, as much separated as connected by digital communications and the information revolution.

But perhaps the most important connection in all these works is the realization that the urban and the natural are no longer in opposition, but exist in a complex continuum. Nature is no longer that which is found, the manmade that which is artificial. We have so altered nature that much of landscape work has to do with restoration, renaturing, and fostering new marine and land environments even as the very climate change mankind has induced is leading nature to change before our eyes. And at the same time, the palette of architectural design has expanded enormously, not only through synthetic materials—some of them even deployed with lessons derived from the study of natural form and processes—but through the increased use of buildings as the underpinnings for a new ecology. Cities are themselves complex ecologies. At least since the 1960s, when Aldo Rossi wrote his poetic and influential *Architecture of the City*, the shaping role of defunct infrastructure in the morphology of cities has made architects aware that the urban nature of found structures created by humans is resonant long after the meaning has been forgotten. And the truism that nature is pristine is no longer a viable fiction. With the current debates over what are called "novel ecosystems"—changed natural systems directly resulting from human intervention, be it the introduction of invasive species or the effects of global warming—comes the recognition that nature, in most areas of intense human occupation, has been altered not only by its own traditionally powerful forces, but also by one of its most willful creations, mankind.

The debate over conservation strategies in the face of these new ecological systems is a hallmark of our current situation. What is offered here by Weiss/Manfredi are suggestive ways in which those very debates resonate in designing the novel ecosystems of today's public infrastructures. To enter the Brooklyn Botanic Garden as they have remodeled it is to experience firsthand, viscerally and visually, the stakes of a debate that refuse precedence—of either nature vs. building in the city, of individual vs. collective in the creation of space for museum education and gatherings amid the strolling paths of the garden, or of architecture vs. landscape design. In Weiss/Manfredi's work in the dense grids of cities, or at the fragile edges of their encounters with larger natural realms, the architects see a blurred territory that becomes for them the petri dish for both new design solutions and new types of public colloquy.

Professor of Art History at Columbia University
Curator at the Museum of Modern Art

Evolutionary Infrastructures

Marion Weiss | Michael A. Manfredi

Infrastructural systems are the enduring forms of urban evolution, multiplying as cities grow and requiring expanding swaths of territory to accommodate more and more monofunctional requirements. As the very momentum of exchange incrementally overwhelms our urban landscapes, we wonder what new forms of public nature might emerge if highways, communication right-of-ways, flood-resistant structures, railways, subway lines, and distribution grids were to become institutions of culture and recreation.

Larger than life but part of it, infrastructure has an immediate presence; it shapes our environment and urban life in vital, authentic, and often messy ways. Tabula-rasa beginnings are rare for cities; hence, infrastructure, of both movement and culture, must evolve and activate preexisting conditions. Highway, subway, utility lines, and teledata networks have the capacity to sever or connect communities, define the static or fluid identity of an urban landscape, and unravel or re-stitch the increasingly fragmented fabric of our metropolitan world. The allure of this new public territory lies in its activation of a range of scales, its sectional opportunities for the simultaneous accommodation of movement and destination, and the hybrid programmatic potentials it affords.

We look at the physical elements of infrastructure and the often marginalized sites they produce as possible contributors to a meaningful public realm. What if a new paradigm for infrastructure existed? What if the very hard lines between landscape, architecture, engineering, and urbanism could find a more synthetic convergence? We are interested in a new model of practice that integrates all fields of design through yet-to-be-codified protocols— a synthesis residing at the periphery of disciplinary definitions but perhaps at the center of a wholly new form.

We imagine a definition for an evolutionary infrastructure that is both projective and pragmatic—an intrinsically agile prototypical ideal, capable of optimizing ecological and social agendas and leveraging the stray spatial consequences of preexisting infrastructures. This definition recognizes that urban centers, particularly those settled in close proximity to water, have experienced great transformation over time. As places of exchange, these cities depended on waterfront infrastructures to facilitate boat and barge traffic, but over time train lines and highways came to facilitate greater speeds of exchange. This evolution of trade and development has resulted in a patchwork layering of infrastructural systems, creating odd juxtapositions and remnant spaces between ports, city grids, train lines, roadways, and highways. Our idea of an evolutionary infrastructure does not condemn the artifacts of infrastructure or depend on an idealized blank-slate condition, but rather envisions new reciprocities between preexisting systems and more ecologically resilient territories suited to contemporary demands.

During periods of rapid urbanization, particularly after World War II, both developed and developing countries built comprehensive networks of roadways and highways to expedite movement within and beyond the core of old cities. Politically fragile communities lacking the strength to protest this signature of progress offered little resistance to such invasive projects. Ecologically fragile waterways and contested landscapes were equally put at risk. The Cross Bronx Expressway in New York divided and devastated its neighborhood, and the Los Angeles Aqueduct system accelerated the creation of deserts to the north and impoverished countless local ecosystems along its way. Once the greatest asset to serve the modern urban landscape, infrastructure has now created cities in perpetual crisis beholden to the seemingly irreconcilable differences between its systems and its objects.

Realizing the limitations of monofunctional infrastructure, we advocate for a more hybrid, resilient, "thick" infrastructure, where large-scale regional ambitions do not preclude programmatic variety, spatial richness, and specificity of detail, but rather suggest an alchemy of innovative engineering, ecological imperatives, and compelling architecture. We envision the necessity of an evolutionary "model for infrastructure"—a public/private model that brings the impatience of the entrepreneurial spirit to the broader collective agendas of public agencies.

Although the Ponte Vecchio in Florence offers an exemplary historic model of program-rich infrastructure, a more idiosyncratic merging of river and urban engineering was realized in Ljubljana, Slovenia, with Jože Plečnik's responsive urban section along the Ljubljanica River. At the heart of the city, his signature triple bridge crosses the river with a spectacle of redundant crossings and delicacy of scale more common in architectural follies than infrastructure. The steep section cut is fortified with stone walls inscribed with stairs, ramps, and arcades, producing a kind of reverse fortification. Outside the urban core, these walls recline at a shallower angle, broadening the width of the river promenade with multilevel walks and water-tolerant trees. The production of this literally sub-urban promenade is both brilliant and subtle. When the river is full, only an upper level walk offers passage; when the water level is low, it follows a slender channel leaving four levels of parallel walkways free for strollers. Between these urban and pastoral states, a series of weirs and bridges create a meter of landmarks along the length of the river. This dynamically changing section accommodates natural events, merging engineering

Ljubljanica River Promenade, by Jože Plečnik, Ljubljana, Slovenia, 1939

Plan Obus for Algiers, by Le
Corbusier, 1933

obligations with ecological agendas, and creating a hardworking
infrastructure that offers a new mode of urban experience.

These very same qualities—programmatic variety and
spatial richness—are part of the legacy of infrastructure-scaled
modernist utopian visions and are a reminder that the legacy of
modernism is complex, and its social motivations often overlooked.
Le Corbusier, with his unrealized designs for Algiers and Rio de
Janeiro, identified a continuous sectional hybrid of highway and
housing. Hugh Ferriss, in his 1929 Metropolis series, described
a vivid dream of a multileveled Manhattan, extended with tendrils
of suspension bridges thick with high-rise apartments embedded
in the supporting pylons. In the decades following World War II,
the Metabolists, principally centered in Japan, rendered a vision
of elevated cities to sustain growing urban centers. These ambitious
proposals, further elaborated in the 1960s in work by Archigram
and Paul Rudolph, anticipate a densely inhabited infrastructure,
capable of supporting multiple layers of urban life.

Though Ferriss's inhabitable infrastructure fantasy was
never realized, an awkward yet extraordinarily contingent utopia
emerged in 1964 at the northern tip of Manhattan. Here, the legacy
of these aspirations took shape in a piecemeal fashion, where the
terminus of the George Washington Bridge translated into the
dramatic cut of the Trans-Manhattan Expressway, expediting
high-speed traffic movement through the city to connect the adjacent boroughs. Topped by Pier Luigi Nervi's inventive bus station
to the west and improbably straddled by four high-rise residential
towers to the east, this unfinished modernist project crosses the
Harlem River and carves through the Bronx with a remnant wake of
on- and off-ramps. This dynamic, yet tragically flawed hybrid was

internationally criticized for destroying the finer-scaled neighbor-
hoods in Manhattan and the Bronx and commingling the exhaust
of cars with the air breathed by the building's low-income tenants.
Although this marriage of infrastructure and inhabitation failed
to become a contemporary paradigm worth reproducing, it was a
bold experiment that prompted the Ford Foundation to commission Rudolph in 1967 to propose an elevated world of highways
and housing crossing though Manhattan, complete with extensive
parking garages and opportunities for residents to enjoy views of
the city while avoiding direct, at grade, engagement with urban life.

      Whereas Manhattan was the focus of both speculative and
realized examples of an inhabitable infrastructure, Brooklyn is
the site of one of the most enduring successes of an infrastructure
hosting speed and slowness, pass-through, and promenade. In the
decade after World War II, urban planner Robert Moses and the
New York City Planning Commission proposed the creation of the
Brooklyn Queens Expressway, an element of progress that would
offer efficient routes through New York City's outer boroughs
that included a cut through the historic brownstone community of
Brooklyn Heights. Led by the Brooklyn Heights Association, the
community countered the plan, and won, with a proposal by
Clarke & Rapuano that cantilevered a two-tiered highway from
the urban bluff with a surface street below. Upon seeing this plan,
Moses reportedly suggested covering this proposal with a public
walk lined with the backyard gardens of the adjacent town houses.
The realized project, opened in 1959, included the now famous
three-eighths mile long promenade, connecting the neighborhood

Brooklyn Heights Promenade,
by Clarke & Rapuano, Brooklyn,
New York, 1959

George Washington Bridge
Bus Terminal, by Pier Luigi Nervi,
New York, 1963

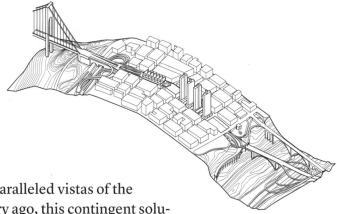

to a shaded urban belvedere with unparalleled vistas of the
Manhattan skyline. Over a half century ago, this contingent solution to a specific challenge offered a sustaining sectional paradigm,
utilizing topography to eliminate the either/or dichotomy associated with urban fabric and infrastructure.

   These heroic infrastructural proposals and seminal projects,
seen through the dual lens of pressing ecological imperatives
and shifting societal patterns, have renewed our interest in the
architectural implication of topography, territory, and urban
systems. The late architectural historian Detlef Mertins suggested
that these types of utopian models offer relevant hybrid, multivalent, and open-ended strategies to consider in contemporary terms.
Against the backdrop of these early inspirational models, we have
been challenged to explore more productive relationships between
infrastructure, ecology, and public life, one where the logistical
obligations of movement and systems are modulated to support
the "plus" of site-specific investment calibrated to the precise
nuances of location and programmatic demand.

   Our preoccupation with a more synthetic potential in these
contested territories has been intensified by experience with
the waterfront cities of Seattle, Toronto, and New York, with sites
almost completely defined by transportation and flooding challenges. In each case, we engaged with projects expressly committed
to expanding the capacity of infrastructure to host new programs
while connecting communities to waterfronts previously defined
by the imposing footprint of industry and transport.

   The Seattle Olympic Sculpture Park, for example, emerged
from the unlikely proposition of turning three separate parcels
of contaminated land, divided by train lines and highways, into

a waterfront public space for the display of art. Segmented in plan and section, the site offered an opportunity to create three separate parks connected by bridges or one monolithic cap to conceal the infrastructure below. We suggested a third alternative— a continuous Z-shaped landform—that alternately concealed and revealed the roadways and train lines below. Within the boundaries of the site's nine acres, the earthwork is shaped to create valleys, bridges, ramps, and walkways, beginning at the urban edge with a pavilion for art and concluding at the water's edge with a newly created beach and underwater habitat "benches" for aquatic life. This pedestrian infrastructure allows long denied free move-ment between downtown Seattle and the waterfront. Beneath the surface plantings of this armature, a new subsurface infrastructure consisting of two and a half miles of power, water, telephone, and data lines allows artists to incorporate sophisticated technolo-gies into their work.

Once an ecologically vibrant river delta, the mouth of the Don River in Toronto was disfigured during the city's industrializa-tion into a concrete channel, terminating the free flow of water to make room for a port, thereby accelerating the cycles of flooding. The addition of the elevated Gardiner Expressway further disrupted this site. Our project for the Lower Don River sought to transform this waterfront into an ecologically engineered setting for public life through the introduction of a more hydrologically sensitive geom-etry of arcs and curves where hard, armored edges gave way to a series of wetlands and walkways. Similarly, in our realized project for Hunter's Point South Waterfront Park, located along New York City's East River, we identified strategies to incorporate the inevi-table and often destructive patterns of flooding, as made evident by the impact of Hurricane Sandy just prior to the project's completion. Here, existing concrete bulkheads are alternately utilized for new elevated landscapes and pavilions, or strategically replaced by new wetlands and paths, creating a soft infrastructural edge. A series of new multiuse open spaces create topographies that accommo-date, rather than oppose, rising waters and fluctuating tidal swells. In each of these cases, an underutilized and forbidding waterfront is given a second life as a resilient and ecological infrastructural system for public use.

In Muju, Korea, the steep slopes and valleys designated for the Taekwondo Park required operating at a territorial scale: larger than architecture but smaller than an urban district. Although initial studies of the site by the South Korean government suggested occupying the site's central valley with buildings and car parks, we elected to preserve the valleys to allow the flow of water, developing a strategy loosely inspired by the contours of the nearby ginseng agricultural terraces. Through merging infrastructural and landscape operations to generate a design at an intermediate scale, we created a sequence of precincts linked by descending water terraces and ascending paths and bridges. In migrating freely from landscape to architecture and back, the project produces a contemporary setting for the competitive and spiritual rituals of Taekwondo.

Although these urban and territorially scaled projects utilize infrastructural strategies to create new public destinations, the evolution of these sensibilities also translates to more compact projects. At the Brooklyn Botanic Garden, an urban oasis in the middle of the city, we designed the new Visitor Center as a linear section connecting city and garden. Nested into an existing hillside, the center is experienced as a three-dimensional continuation of the garden path system, hosting spaces for exhibitions and events and creating a new green rooftop garden. Pathways cross through the building at an upper level, and the project's landscaped surfaces create an ambiguous boundary between garden and architectural space. An inhabitable and seasonally variable topography, the Center serves as an interface between city and garden, culture and cultivation.

The sensibilities of infrastructure and the project of architecture are latent with reciprocities yet to be imagined. Although infrastructure is often incorrectly perceived as hard and inflexible, we see great potential for alternative strategies that structure more lateral, resilient, and pliable systems capable of hosting unpredictable uses and activities, absorbing cycles of flooding, accommodating variable traffic volumes, and generating cultural value. By bending the loose ends of architecture, landscape, and engineering together, we imagine an alchemy that transcends the limitations of single-use infrastructures, generating a more bountiful and inhabitable interpretation of its potential.

Evolutionary Infrastructures

Seattle Art Museum: Olympic Sculpture Park
Toronto Lower Don Lands
Hunter's Point South Waterfront Park
Taekwondo Park
Brooklyn Botanic Garden Visitor Center

Seattle Art Museum: Olympic Sculpture Park

Seattle, Washington

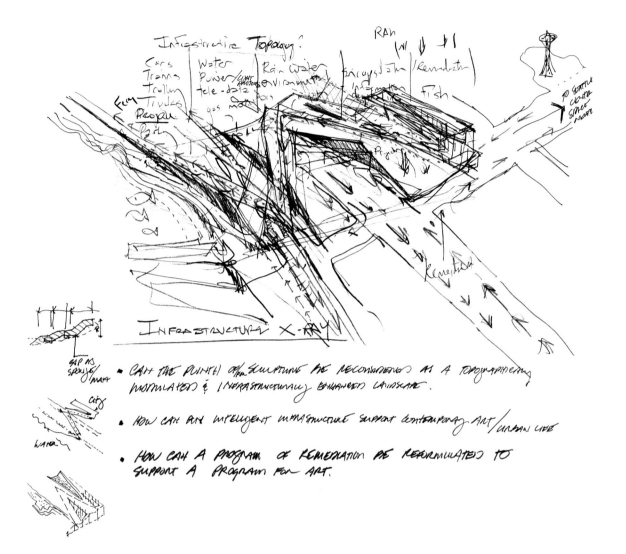

Denny Regrade

In Seattle's first hundred years of urban settlement, the steep waterfront bluff was radically altered by a series of regrading projects. The regrading of Denny Hill dramatically changed the natural topography of the Olympic Sculpture Park site. Inspired by this early history, the park design amplifies the topographic evolution of the site.

Graced with a bounty of natural advantages, Seattle has long sought to balance its innate ecological value with its growing appetite for innovation and alternative modes of urban life. From its earliest days as a logging and commercial shipbuilding center to its current position at the forefront of the digital commerce and sustainable development industries, the city persists as an experimental space within a dramatic geography defined by Mt. Rainier, the Cascades, and Puget Sound.

While postindustrial Seattle had its sights set on software development and fostering digital exchange, its physical landscape remained marred by the infrastructural legacy of its past industrial prosperity, which had effectively severed the city from its waterfront. The visual impression of continuity achieved between Seattle's urban and natural environments from the height of the Space Needle remained a fiction on the ground. In a bid to reclaim and restore the city's waterfront, the Seattle Art Museum's Olympic Sculpture Park hoped to circumvent the typical relationship of art behind the museum walls and offer a radical alternative: art and design as part of the public realm.

The site chosen for the international design competition existed as three individual parcels separated from the water by the city's existing infrastructural networks. Weaving together these distinct sites, the 8.5-acre park operates as a hybrid landform that provides a new pedestrian infrastructure and reunites the city with its shore-line. Streams of visitors populate the terracing lawns at the capped site of a former Unocal fuel storage and transfer station, which hosts an average of 450,000 visitors per year.

Three Distinct Sites
Three former industrial sites located between downtown Seattle and Elliott Bay were separated by roadways and rail lines. The design strategy connects these sites and forms a continuous topography that descends forty feet (12 m) from the city to a newly created beach.

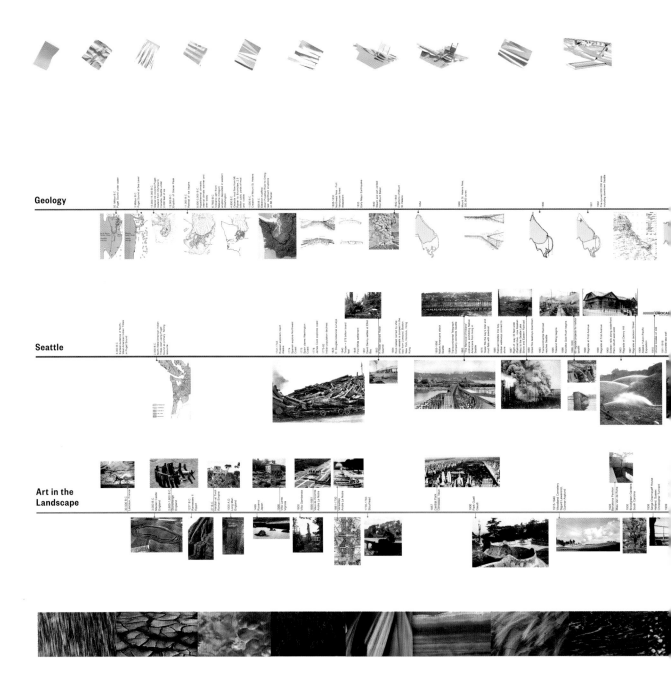

Geology

Seattle

Art in the
Landscape

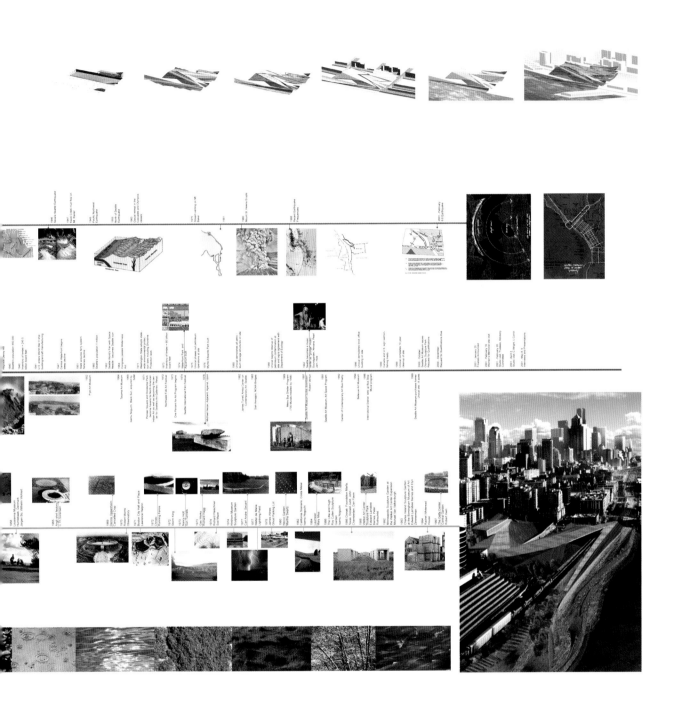

260,000 cubic yards (198,784 m³)
of earth were sculpted to
create the landforms that define
the connecting topography.

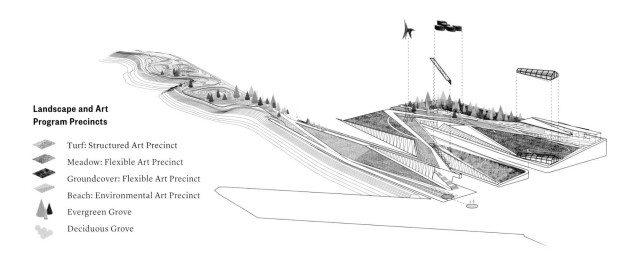

**Landscape and Art
Program Precincts**

Turf: Structured Art Precinct

Meadow: Flexible Art Precinct

Groundcover: Flexible Art Precinct

Beach: Environmental Art Precinct

Evergreen Grove

Deciduous Grove

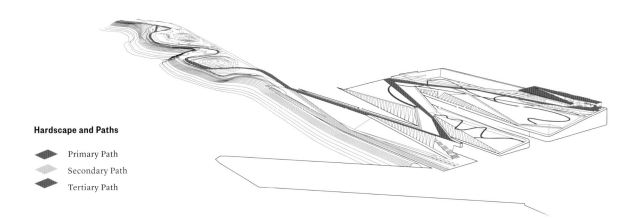

Hardscape and Paths

Primary Path

Secondary Path

Tertiary Path

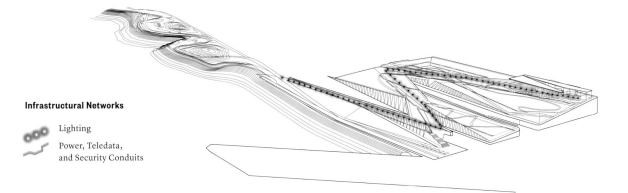

Infrastructural Networks

Lighting

Power, Teledata,
and Security Conduits

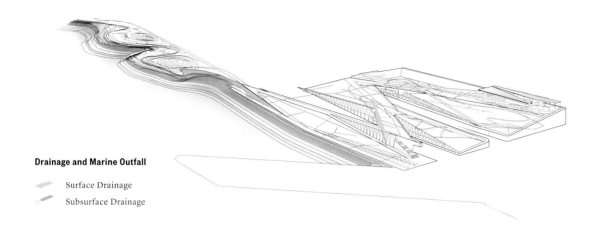

Drainage and Marine Outfall

Surface Drainage

Subsurface Drainage

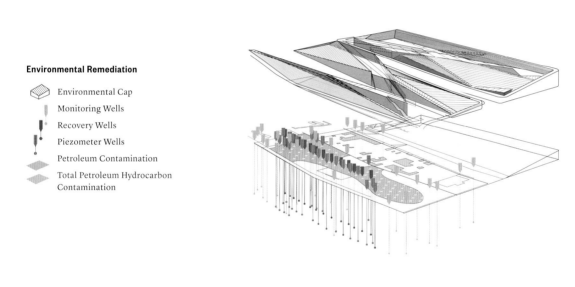

Environmental Remediation

Environmental Cap

Monitoring Wells

Recovery Wells

Piezometer Wells

Petroleum Contamination

Total Petroleum Hydrocarbon
Contamination

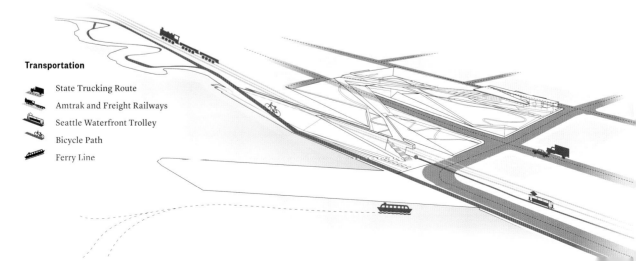

Transportation

State Trucking Route

Amtrak and Freight Railways

Seattle Waterfront Trolley

Bicycle Path

Ferry Line

The park vaults over a site sliced into three parcels by train tracks and a four-lane arterial road separating downtown Seattle from Elliott Bay, and unfolds as a continuous Z-shaped landscape that wanders from the city to the water, alternately revealing and concealing the train tracks and roadways below. A new ecological infrastructure is layered over the existing site with a system of mechanically stabilized earth and capitalizes on the forty-foot grade change to the water's edge.

The enhanced earthwork reestablishes the original topography of the site in a chameleonlike approach that begins as a fully emerged form—a hilltop pavilion—and concludes in a fully submerged condition—a shoreline garden. In an effort to rethink the conventions of the typical sculpture park, the Olympic Sculpture Park provides a dynamic and evolving setting for art, implicitly questioning where the park begins and the art ends.

The rhythm of slipped concrete retaining walls, infrastructural in scale, provides a metering device that links architecture, earthwork, landscape, and art. These concrete retaining walls run along the park's meadows, where its overlapping panels are engineered to anticipate future seismic shifts in the region.

The landform's alternating tilting planes create
settings for diverse ecological environments,
weaving visitors through distinctly different landscape precincts. Throughout the park, landforms
and plantings collaborate to direct, collect, and
cleanse storm water as it moves through the site
before being released into the bay.

Art, landscape, and infrastructure are superimposed over existing urban systems to meet distinctly different demands. The landform's chameleonlike section reveals its multiple roles: to elevate the pavilion, cross a highway, bridge over train tracks, and reshape the waterfront.

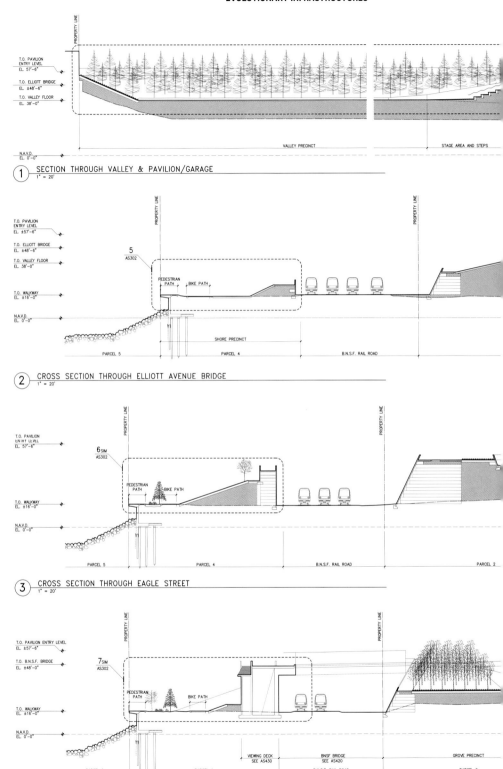

1 SECTION THROUGH VALLEY & PAVILION/GARAGE
1" = 20'

2 CROSS SECTION THROUGH ELLIOTT AVENUE BRIDGE
1" = 20'

3 CROSS SECTION THROUGH EAGLE STREET
1" = 20'

4 CROSS SECTION THROUGH PAVILION & ALASKAN WAY ENTRY PLAZA
1" = 20'

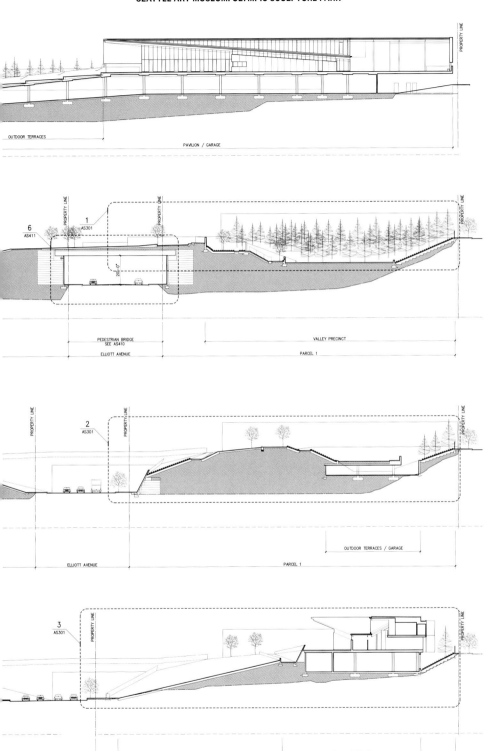

OUTDOOR TERRACES

PAVILION / GARAGE

6
AS411

1
AS301

PROPERTY LINE

PROPERTY LINE

PROPERTY LINE

20'-0"

PEDESTRIAN BRIDGE
SEE AS410

VALLEY PRECINCT

ELLIOTT AVENUE

PARCEL 1

PROPERTY LINE

2
AS301

PROPERTY LINE

PROPERTY LINE

OUTDOOR TERRACES / GARAGE

ELLIOTT AVENUE

PARCEL 1

3
AS301

PROPERTY LINE

PROPERTY LINE

EAST MEADOW

PAVILION / GARAGE

ELLIOTT AVENUE

PARCEL 1

Mechanically Stabilized Earth (MSE)

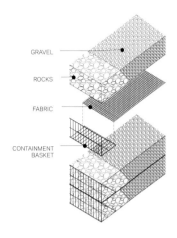

GRAVEL

ROCKS

FABRIC

CONTAINMENT
BASKET

MSE Wall

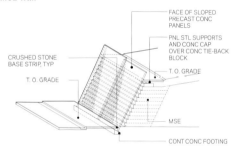

CRUSHED STONE
BASE STRIP, TYP

T. O. GRADE

FACE OF SLOPED
PRECAST CONC
PANELS

PNL STL SUPPORTS
AND CONC CAP
OVER CONC TIE-BACK
BLOCK

T. O. GRADE

MSE

CONT CONC FOOTING

Salmonoid Beach Habitat

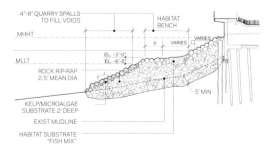

4"-8" QUARRY SPALLS
TO FILL VOIDS

HABITAT
BENCH

MHHT

VARIES

6'   VARIES

EL. -3'-0"
EL. -6'-0"

MLLT

ROCK RIP-RAP
2.5' MEAN DIA

5' MIN

KELP/MICROALGAE
SUBSTRATE 2' DEEP

EXIST MUDLINE

HABITAT SUBSTRATE
"FISH MIX"

Pavilion Excavation

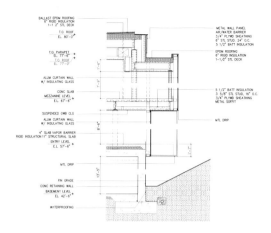

Structural MSE at Elliott Bridge

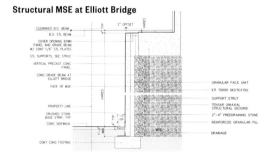

Battered MSE at Road and Train Track

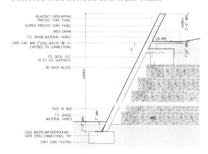

Vertical MSE at Train Bridge

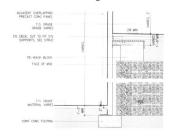

The project's visual profile appears to give way to the landscape as the cascading pathway unfurls with a new shoreline at the bay. The shore echoes the Pacific Northwest pocket beach in feel and appearance, reinforced with riprap rock and planted with native dune grasses.

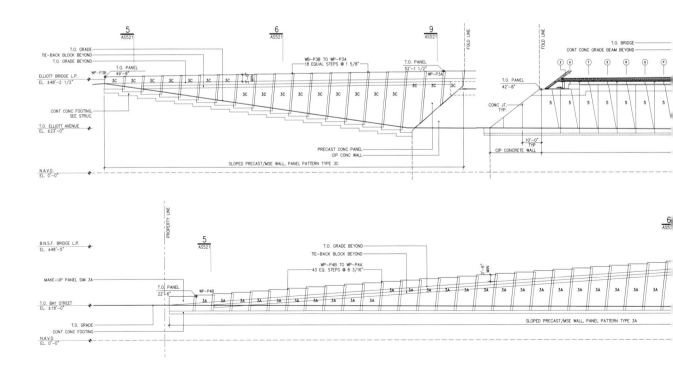

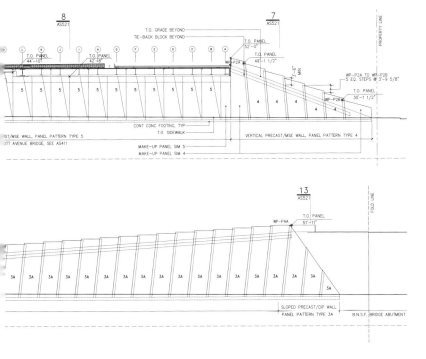

At the top of the park, the exhibition pavilion unfolds from the landscape, providing spaces for art, performances, and educational programming. Between skyline and water, visitors engage the pavilion's stepped amphitheater before the undulating Cor-ten slabs of Richard Serra's "Wake," which rise from the gravel floor of the valley precinct below.

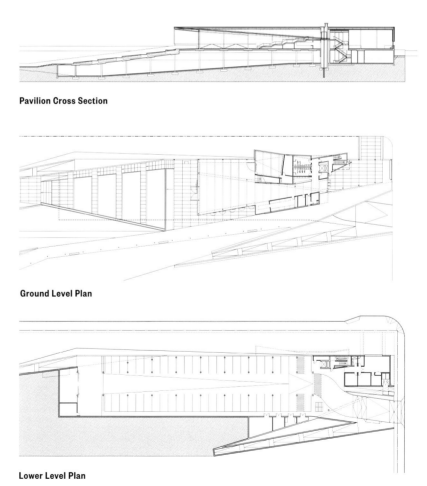

Pavilion Cross Section

Ground Level Plan

Lower Level Plan

One of several pieces of art commissioned or acquired specifically for the site, "Wake" is joined by Louise Bourgeois's "Father and Son," Alexander Calder's "Eagle," and Mark di Suvero's "Schubert Sonata," as some of the primary anchors in the park's evolving collection. Another piece, "Seattle Cloud Cover" by Teresita Fernández is a site-specific artwork of luminous glass seamlessly integrated into the park's railway bridge. Mark Dion's "Neukom Vivarium," offers a hybrid work of sculpture and horticultural education in its display within a greenhouse-inspired pavilion sited at the park's Elliott Avenue and Broad Street entrance, one of many points of entry that blur the edge between park and city. A microscopic theater of decay and renewal, the sixty-foot hemlock nursing log removed from the Olympic Forest supports the park's aim of celebrating the integration of art and ecology.

The spine of the park, the promenade, thickens
this traditionally scenographic and monofunctional
device into an armature for art, recreation, and
environmental remediation. Performance requires
an effective form, both in gesture and detail.
As the path establishes a series of relationships
at one scale, the edges of the park enable a number
of others across a range of scales for inhabitants.

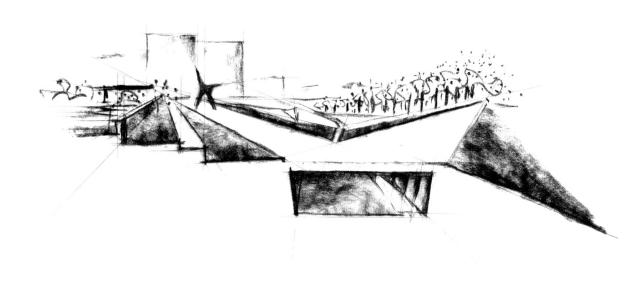

A new public promenade creates a bike and running trail along Elliott Bay to enhance public access to Puget Sound. Here, works by Louise Bourgeois, Roy McMakin, and Mark di Suvero are featured.

This newly designed beach encourages biodiversity on a site previously damaged by petrochemical waste. Designed with aquatic terraces that form a subtidal safe haven for a juvenile salmon marine habitat, the new shoreline establishes the only habitat of its kind on Seattle's urban waterfront.

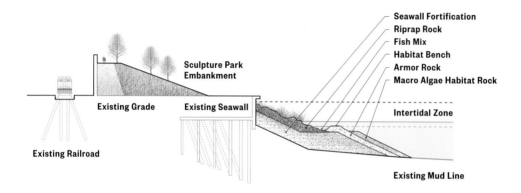

Seawall Fortification
Riprap Rock
Fish Mix
Habitat Bench
Armor Rock
Macro Algae Habitat Rock

Sculpture Park Embankment

Existing Grade

Existing Seawall

Intertidal Zone

Existing Railroad

Existing Mud Line

In reshaping the waterfront, the park stabilized a damaged seawall and created a nearshore habitat as refuge for salmon migration in the Puget Sound estuary. In less than a decade this modest habitat bench has led to a 500 percent increase in the local Chinook salmon population.

Taking on a life of its own, both ecologically and socially, the character of the park continues to evolve as its initial formal interventions encourage new forms of improvisation. The park plays host to a layering of programs throughout the year— food trucks line the paths of the park, bands play in the valley, yoga classes engage the amphitheater, and museum curators lead walking tours and drawing classes. The park is an increasingly active public space that provides an adaptable infrastructure for a range of social uses and exchange, from the informal urban dweller (biker, jogger, dog walker) to the staged event (farmer's market, concert, wedding).

As a landscape for art, the Olympic Sculpture Park defines a new experience for modern and contemporary art outside the museum walls. Illuminating the power of an invented landscape to create connections between art and ecology, city and waterfront, the deliberately open-ended design invites new interpretations for art, ecology, and urban engagement.

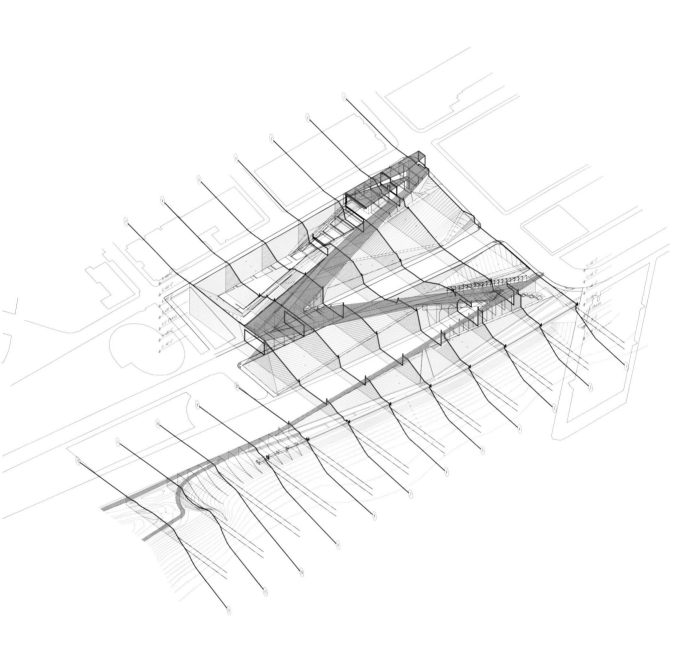

Toronto Lower Don Lands

Toronto, Ontario

Before Toronto was first settled, in 1787, the Don
Watershed released into Lake Ontario through
Ashbridge's Bay, the largest wetland in southeast
Canada. As Toronto grew, industry transformed the
mouth of the Don River into a concrete landscape,
terminating the free flow of water to make room
for an industrial port. Roadways, expressways, and
overpasses now span the Don, concealing a nature
that once sustained a vital ecosystem. Today,
the Lower Don Lands represent a void in the eastern
part of Toronto that disconnects the Don River
Greenway from the emerging waterfront. In response
to an invitation to participate in an international
competition to reintegrate the three hundred acre
site with the developing waterfront of downtown
Toronto and provide a more natural terminus for
the Don River, a system of wandering ecologies is
proposed in which recreational, living, and cultural
activities overlap with new hydrological and green
infrastructures.

Flooding
The most severe flood in Canadian history occurred in 1954 when Hurricane Hazel raised water levels by twenty feet (6m) in the Don River.

Industrial Heritage
The waterfront zone has left a legacy of Toronto's industrial past.

Barriers
The site is transected by a series of highway interchanges.

Floodplain

Existing Condition

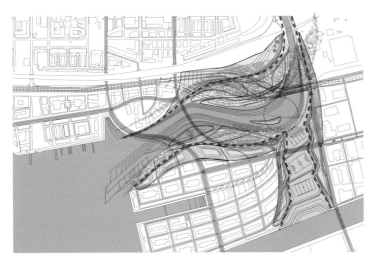

10-Year Floodplain

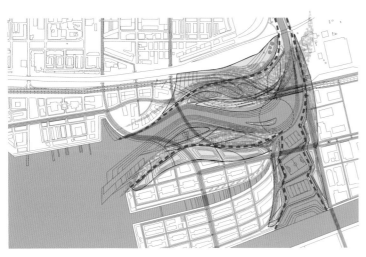

100-Year Floodplain

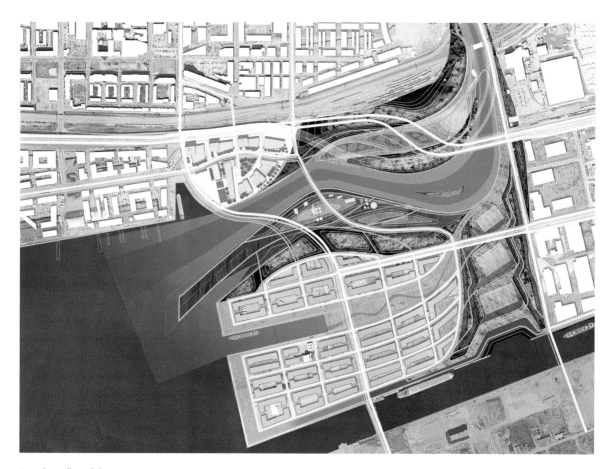

A newly configured river
hydrology relaxes the flood-
prone edge of the river channel
with a resilient geometry that
accommodates the inevitable
flooding of the site.

Channelized to allow for port activity, the altered
mouth of the Don River has long been inhospitable
to avian and aquatic life and maintains little reciprocity with the urban life of present-day Toronto.
With optimal waterfront access and unimpeded
views of the city's skyline, the site is uniquely
positioned to double as a new residential center
and a recreational destination.

A New Flood Release Channel
A constructed valley of terraced playing fields establishes a new recreational zone and provides a spillway to accommodate flooding.

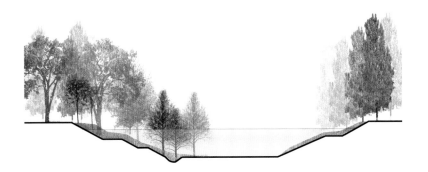

Expanding on the design objectives posited in Seattle, the project creates a public waterfront park directly on Lake Ontario to accommodate a range of uses and offer an approach to flood control that works with the site rather than against it. The proposal, named "Wandering Ecologies," aims to support multiple natures where activities such as kayaking and fishing benefit from the introduction of new wetlands and wildlife habitats within the fabric of the city.

Contaminated fill is removed to create a new wetland ecology layered with a network of elevated boardwalks that introduce a new recreational infrastructure.

Connected to the downtown through a network of routes that accommodate public transit, parkways, local roads, bicycle trails, and an extensive pedestrian network, the site also links a series of new public park spaces and beaches along the southern bank of the Don River through a meandering path that culminates in a boardwalk and pier overlook. The overlook is the focal point of the park and offers a year-round setting for events against a dramatic backdrop that provides access and views of the downtown. More fundamentally, however, the engagement with the section of the site goes beyond the provision of views. Circulation paths populate the underutilized area around elevated highways that cross the site.

A sunken valley on the site's eastern edge functions both as a series of recreational fields for organized sports and a flood spillway for the Don River, protecting the surrounding residential neighborhood and sensitive ecological habitats along the river's mouth. The proposed transformation of the Lower Don Lands unlocks the site's potential to be naturalized through artifice and humanized by nature, providing a critical prototype for the innovative development of languishing postindustrial districts within otherwise vibrant cities. This new public waterfront for the city of Toronto is a catalyst for urban development which celebrates multiple ecologies: city and water, infrastructure and ecology, destination and retreat.

Section through Marshlands

Section through Peninsula

Section through Pier

Section through Recreational Valley

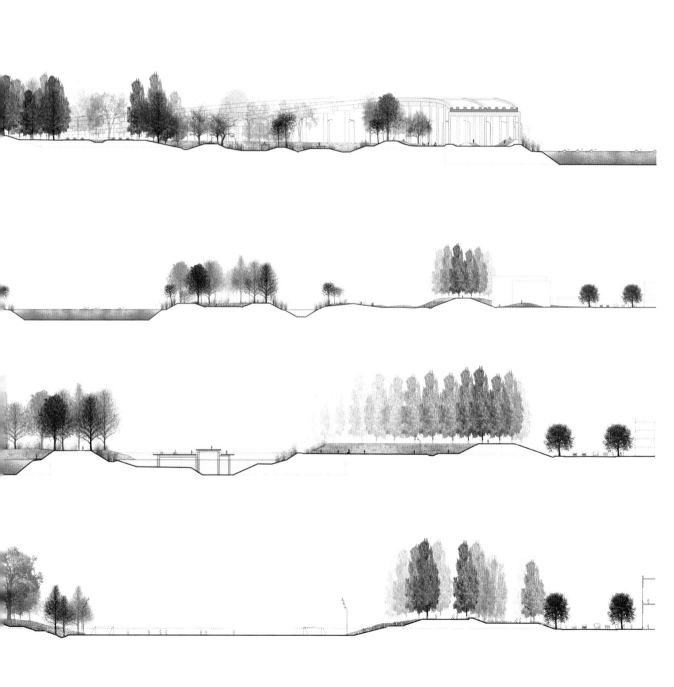

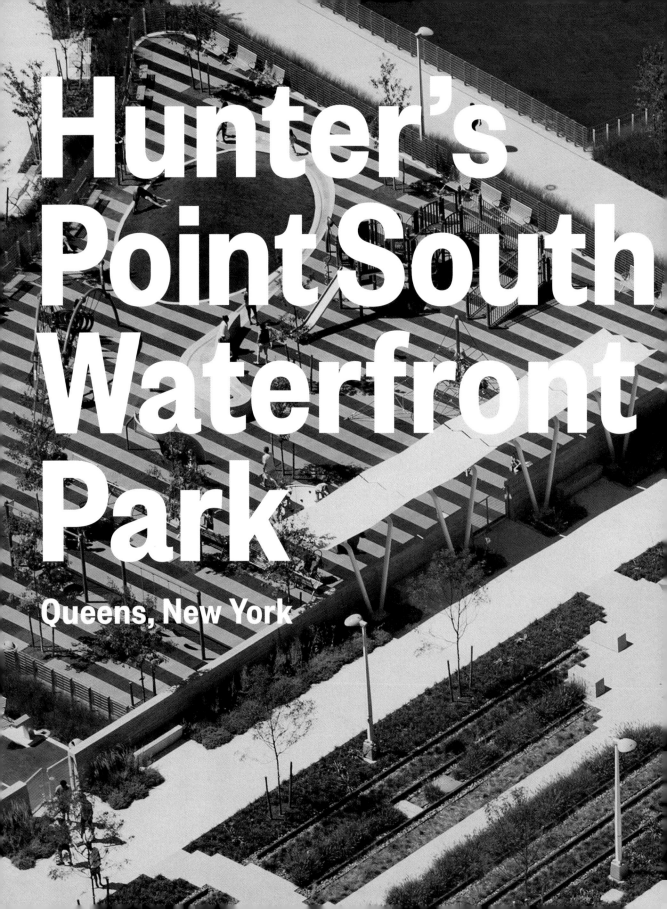

Hunter's Point South Waterfront Park

Queens, New York

In 2012, as Hurricane Sandy flooded the low-lying areas of New York and turned off the lights in Lower Manhattan, Long Island City was hit by a four-foot storm surge that consumed the then-under-construction grounds of Hunter's Point South Waterfront Park. Though built above New York's one-hundred-year floodplain in the hope of avoiding such an onslaught, the park was designed to withstand a trial by water and act as a protective perimeter for the neighboring residential community. As floodwaters receded, the grounds gradually drained the remaining water back into the East River, easing the burden on the city's overtaxed sewer system. Its infrastructures and surfaces intact, the park was completed and opened less than a year later.

Designed in collaboration with Thomas Balsley Associates and Arup, the park was conceived as a resilient waterfront edge, transforming thirty acres of postindustrial waterfront in Queens into a program-rich public space that serves the Long Island City community. Surrounded by water on three sides, the design incorporates numerous sustainable initiatives, converting a strategically located but underutilized waterfront plagued by chronic disinvestment into a new urban ecological model capable of anticipating the cultural needs of a dense residential development as well as the long-term challenges posed by sea-level rise.

Two hundred years ago the site was a series of wetlands. A more recent industrial identity reflects its strategic proximity to waterfront and rail exchange, eliminating all signs of its early ecologically rich history. Today, this legacy presents a paradox—the park leverages its layered histories and spectacular views to establish a new resilient, multilayered recreational and cultural destination. The design proposed a series of parallel perimeter ecologies that link the northern and southern ends of the site.

These linear strands form new ecological corridors that run parallel to the water's edge, providing multiple systems of paths that link the major precincts and programs of the park. Along the water, existing concrete bulkheads were strategically replaced with new wetlands and paths to create an infrastructurally "soft" edge. The park's highly irregular perimeter varies widely from slender to broad widths of land between the city and water, influencing the scale of program elements throughout the park.

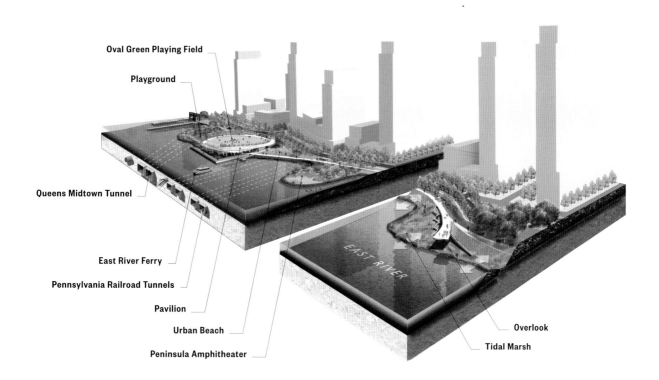

Oval Green Playing Field

Playground

Queens Midtown Tunnel

East River Ferry

Pennsylvania Railroad Tunnels

Pavilion

Urban Beach

Peninsula Amphitheater

EAST RIVER

Overlook

Tidal Marsh

Fluctuating Conditions

A historically rich site, Hunter's Point South Waterfront Park has evolved from a marshy wetland to a drained landfill site, from a soft shoreline to an armored water's edge. The site's dramatic views, rich industrial heritage, and emergent ecologies define its legacy.

Five thousand new units of housing are planned for the neighborhood, making Hunter's Point the largest affordable housing building project in metropolitan New York since the 1970s. Here, the city has inverted the conventional development process in which existing infrastructures are forced to respond to the introduction of new towers, absorbing a huge influx in population. At Hunter's Point, the first phase of the park opened in tandem with a new school—providing a new cultural fabric in advance of the construction of the first towers. Further embracing this sequence, the 9.5-acre northern precinct of the park is designed as a heavily programmed space that accommodates a greater amount of daily use than the more passive landscape of the park's second phase to the south.

Moving south along the waterfront, an urban dog run frames an interpretive rail garden, where a diverse palette of native grasses envelop freight rails, recalling the site's industrial past. From there, a playground, adult fitness space, and basketball courts lead to an oval lawn at the widest portion of the site. The multiuse green oval is split into a circular green surfaced with artificial turf, actively used by the neighboring school as a soccer field, and a raised outer crescent planted with natural grass. Juxtaposing natural and artificial, the two-tiered lawn accommodates varying intensities of use.

1   **Net Zero Solar Lighting**
Photovoltaic panels on the pavilion roof feed energy
to the grid, offsetting annual energy consumption.

2   **Bioretention Swale**
Water is channeled through biofiltration subsoils that
remediate and detain storm water before it reaches
the East River, improving water quality and reducing
flood risks.

3   **Passive Ventilation**
The pavilion's orientation and minimal footprint reduces
the need for temperature conditioning systems.

4   **Kebonized Wood Decking**
Southern yellow pine treated with sugarcane biowaste
has the durability of tropical hardwoods without releasing
harmful by-products or threatening endangered forests.

5   **Natural and Synthetic Grass**
A low-upkeep synthetic turf used within the oval allows
yearlong use without irrigation or maintenance, and
natural grass outside the oval supports other uses.

6   **Multimodal Transportation Initiatives**
The pavilion shelters a ferry connection to Manhattan,
and the park extends New York City's Bicycle Network
Development Program with new lanes and a walking
and jogging circuit.

7   **Native Plant Communities**
A palette of native and regionally appropriate plant
communities that are resilient to drought and inundation
eliminates the need for extensive irrigation.

8   **Storm Surge Anticipation**
The oval, peninsula, and tidal marshlands are designed
to withstand inundation. Four feet (1 m) of water
was drained from the site after Hurricane Sandy with
minimal impact.

9   **Sustainable Streetscape**
New street infrastructure creates a vegetated buffer
zone of trees and green spaces to help slow runoff
and reduce the city's carbon footprint.

10   **Permeable Surfaces**
Crushed stone pathways, riprap slopes, and a sandy
beach provide heat-reflective, water-absorbent surfaces
that minimize storm runoff.

11   **High Marsh Mitigation Zone**
Wetland marshes manage tidal fluctuations and
adapt to changing water levels to restore natural patterns
of the riverside environment.

12   **Riparian Walk**
An inhabitable breakwater balanced between river
and marsh reinvigorates the formerly industrial
waterfront with a new, soft edge that displays an
innovative urban ecology.

Phase two of the park features a
cantilevered overlook, suspended
thirty feet (9 m) over new wetlands
at the southern terminus of the site.

Existing Bluff

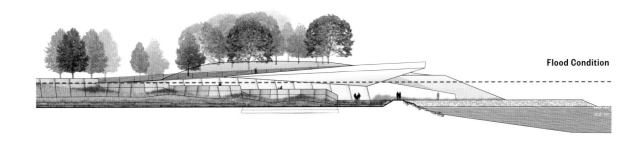

Flood Condition

The urban-scaled ambitions of the Hunter's Point
South development are supported by a careful
layering of resilient materials and systems designed
for durability and self-sufficiency. Shaped by
a tapered concrete ring of seating, the lawn is the
programmatic and sustainable core of the park,
primed to receive floodwater inundation and
mitigate its spread.

100-Year Flood Condition

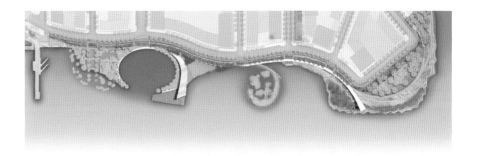

Within the park, precast concrete sections serve dual purpose as a ring of seating and a defensive water barrier at the lawn. Throughout the park, a waterfront boardwalk and integrated seating elements are surfaced with kebonized southern yellow pine, a pre-treatment process that makes the material capable of weathering water inundation and a range of environmental conditions.

Typical Condition

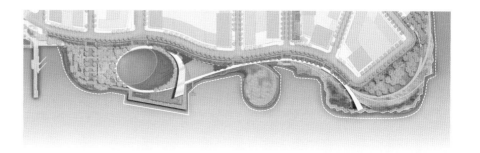

1. Base geometry and grid extracted from site context

2. Projection of base curves

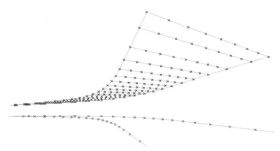

3. Beams connect key points

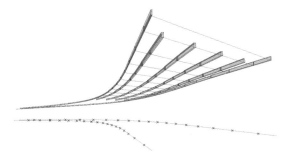

4. Cross beams follow grid lines

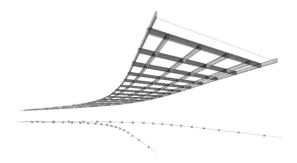

5. Columns connect vertical cross points

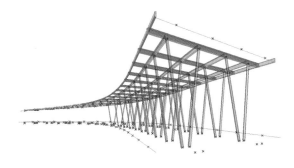

6. Folded surface panels unify segments

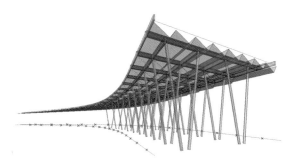

7. Building footprint follows geometry of canopy above

8. A new integrated park pavilion

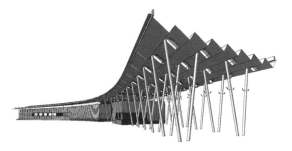

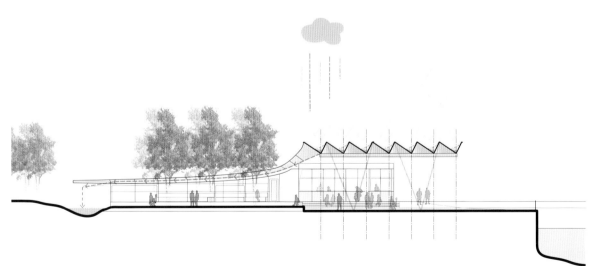

Program-Rich Pavilion
The pavilion functions simultaneously as a new ferry shelter, shade structure, Department of Parks and Recreation office, and café.

Solar Collecting Roof
A bank of photovoltaic panels affixed to the pavilion roof generates enough power to meet over half of the park's demands.

Expanded Pedestrian Network
In addition to sheltering a ferry stop, the park extends New York City's Bicycle Network Development Program with new lanes and a walking and running circuit.

Water Collecting Roof
Roof valleys collect water to nourish plants in the adjacent landscape.

A curved pavilion frames the southern edge of the lawn and extends to form a pleated steel canopy, providing shade for an outdoor café and framing a powerful view across the river to the Empire State Building. Inflecting the larger urban infrastructures of the city, new avenues radiate outward from the park. These "green streets" are integrated with plantings, benches, accessible bike paths, and porous paving with subsurface infrastructures that allow for the sustainable collection of water runoff. This layered approach to streets and sidewalks advocates for a new form of hybrid pedestrian infrastructure within the city.

The intersection between the city and the park is further defined by a richly planted bioswale and gabion ledge absorbing rainwater and resisting the force of potential floodwaters. Absent an irrigation system, the park is planted with native, salt-tolerant species such as coastal little bluestem, seaside goldenrod, and purple coneflower, which can survive an encounter with brackish river water.

A sand-covered beach completes the first phase and overlooks a landing for the East River Ferry, tying into a larger connective loop of the Manhattan, Brooklyn, and Queens waterfronts. This innovative and integrated design collectively offers an international model for innovative waterfront development, creating a new sustainable strategy that weaves infrastructure, landscape, and architecture, bringing the city to the park and the park to the waterfront.

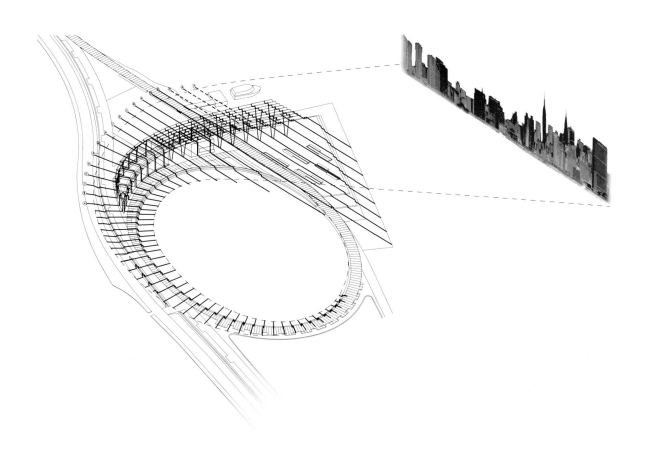

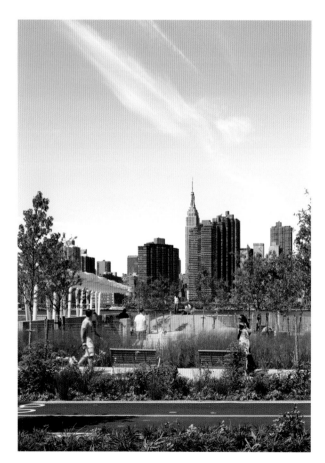

Zones of Activity
Phase one of the park was
designed to be actively
programmed with recreational
amenities that support the
surrounding community. An
ensemble of play venues for
all ages includes basketball
courts, an urban dog run, and
a children's playground.

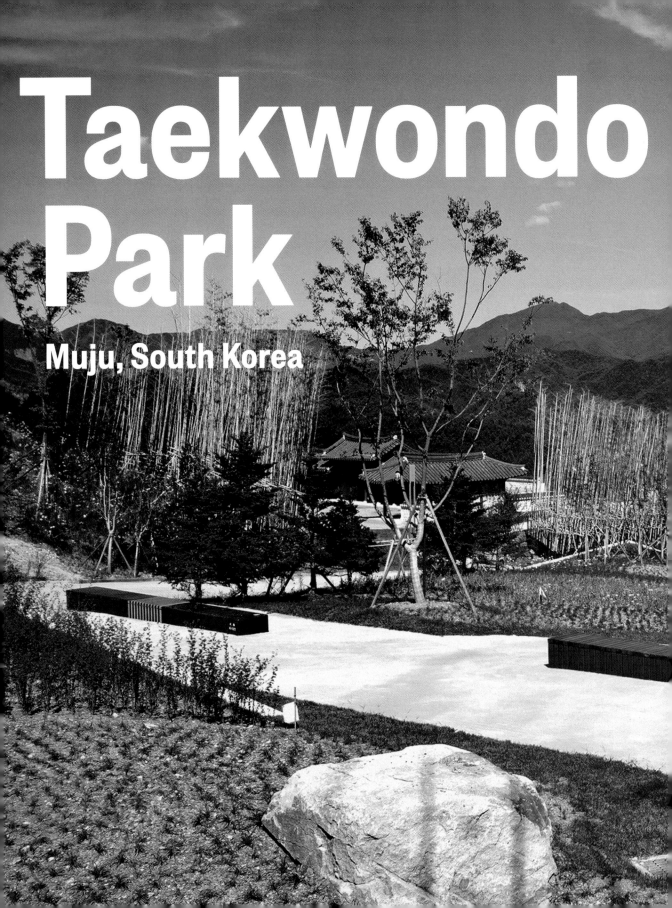

Taekwondo Park

Muju, South Korea

In the Korean martial art of Taekwondo, training is a layered journey of combat, self-defense, and philosophical balance. In this loop of physical training and mental reflection is an ethos that supports cultivation across all forms, blurring the distinction between mind, body, and spirit. Throughout Taekwondo Park, the distinction between building and site is blurred. A commission by the Taekwondo Promotion Foundation of Korea to design a place of gathering to further the practice and experience of the martial art, the park brings together multiple activities, views, and landscape elements in a setting that embodies the philosophical principles of Taekwondo.

Envisioned to serve as the iconic center for the seventy million practitioners of Taekwondo around the world, the park is organized around an ascending path composed of three distinct precincts that symbolically represent body, mind, and spirit. Nestled within the mountainous landscape of Muju, the design builds on the topography of the existing site and heightens its sequence of movement by strategically placing buildings, paths, and bridges throughout the topographically challenging landscape.

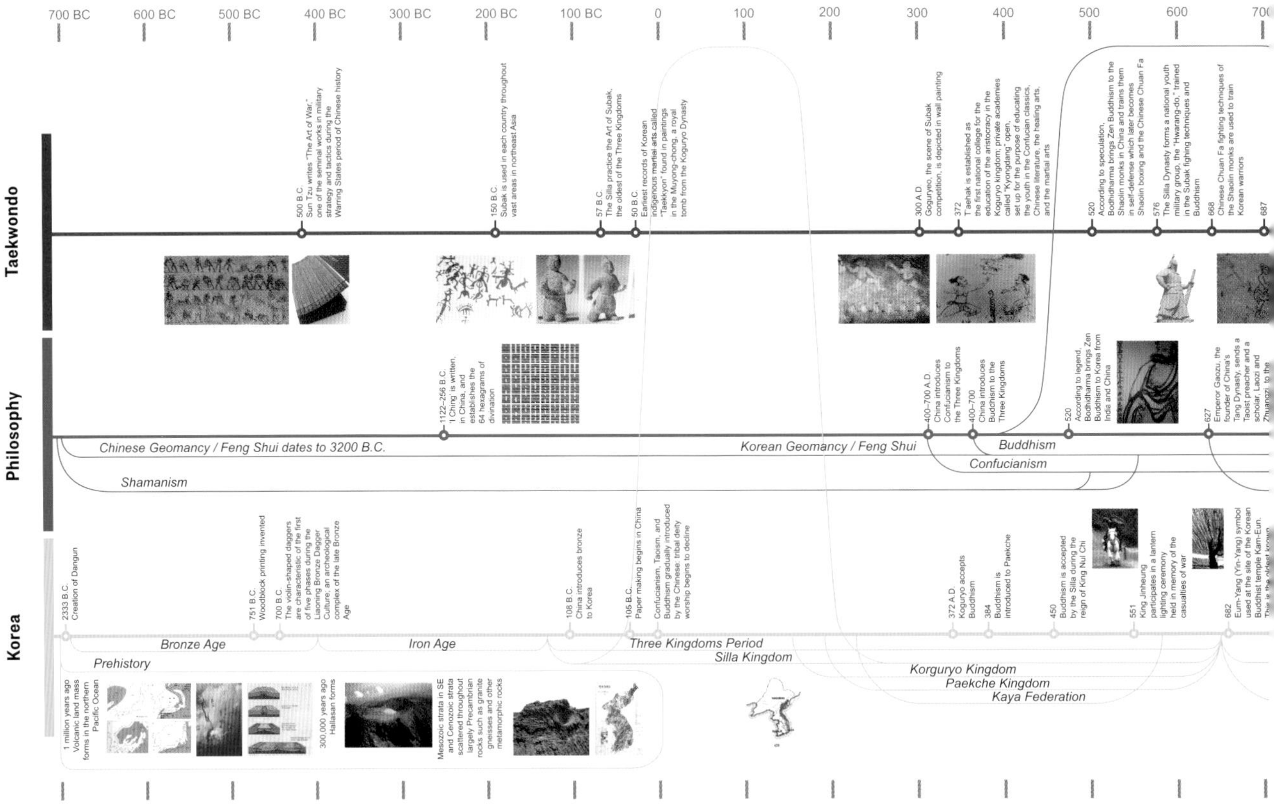
700 BC
600 BC
500 BC
400 BC
300 BC
200 BC
100 BC
0
100
200
300
400
500
600
70
Taekwondo
500 B.C. Sun Tzu writes "The Art of War," one of the seminal works in military strategy and tactics during the Warring States period of Chinese history
150 B.C. Subak is used in each country throughout vast areas in northeast Asia
57 B.C. The Silla practice the Art of Subak, the oldest of the Three Kingdoms
50 B.C. Earliest records of Korean indigenous martial arts called "Taekkyon" found in paintings in the Muyong-chong, a royal tomb from the Koguryo Dynasty
300 A.D. Goguryeo, the scene of Subak competition, is depicted in wall painting
372 Taehak is established as the first national college for the education of the aristocracy in the Koguryo kingdom; private academies called "Kyongdang" open, set up for the purpose of educating the youth in the Confucian classics, Chinese literature, the healing arts, and the martial arts
520 According to speculation, Bodhidharma brings Zen Buddhism to the Shaolin monks in China and trains them in self-defense which later becomes Shaolin boxing and the Chinese Chuan Fa
576 The Silla Dynasty forms a national youth military group, the "Hwarang-do," trained in the Subak fighting techniques and Buddhism
668 Chinese Chuan Fa fighting techniques of the Shaolin monks are used to train Korean warriors
687
Philosophy
1122–256 B.C. 'I Ching' is written, in China, and establishes the 64 hexagrams of divination
400–700 A.D. China introduces Confucianism to the Three Kingdoms
400–700 China introduces Buddhism to the Three Kingdoms
520 According to legend, Bodhidharma brings Zen Buddhism to Korea from India and China
627 Emperor Gaozu, the founder of China's Tang Dynasty, sends a Taoist preacher and a scholar, Laozi and Zhuangzi, to the
Chinese Geomancy / Feng Shui dates to 3200 B.C.
Korean Geomancy / Feng Shui
Buddhism
Confucianism
Shamanism
Korea
2333 B.C. Creation of Dangun
751 B.C. Woodblock printing invented
700 B.C. The violin-shaped daggers are characteristic of the first of five phases during the Liaoning Bronze Dagger Culture, an archeological complex of the late Bronze Age
108 B.C. China introduces bronze to Korea
105 B.C. Paper making begins in China
Confucianism, Taoism, and Buddhism gradually introduced by the Chinese: tribal deity worship begins to decline
372 A.D. Koguryo accepts Buddhism
384 Buddhism is introduced to Paekche
450 Buddhism is accepted by the Silla during the reign of King Nul Chi
551 King Jinheung participates in a lantern lighting ceremony held in memory of the casualties of war
682 Eum-Yang (Yin-Yang) symbol used at the site of the Korean Buddhist temple Kam-Eun. This is the oldest known
Bronze Age
Iron Age
Prehistory
Three Kingdoms Period
Silla Kingdom
Korguryo Kingdom
Paekche Kingdom
Kaya Federation
1 million years ago Volcanic land mass forms in the northern Pacific Ocean
300,000 years ago Hallasan forms
Mesozoic strata in SE and Cenozoic strata scattered throughout largely Precambrian rocks such as granite gneisses and other metamorphic rocks

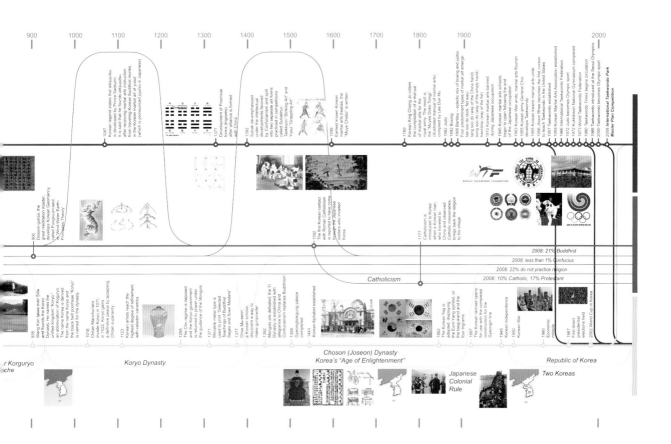

900 1000 1100 1200 1300 1400 1500 1600 1700 1800 1900 2000

Catholicism

2008: 21% Buddhist

2008: less than 1% Confucius

2008: 22% do not practice religion

2008: 10% Catholic, 17% Protestant

r Korguryo
che

Koryo Dynasty

Choson (Joseon) Dynasty
Korea's "Age of Enlightenment"

Republic of Korea

Japanese
Colonial
Rule

Two Koreas

Organized in three precincts, the armature of the design has the ability to evolve over time and accommodate a vast array of activities. The first precinct, the Body, resides at the lowest elevation of the site and includes an arrival plaza and arena. The second precinct, the Mind, at the intermediate elevation, includes research and training centers, which form an amphitheater of terraced buildings that look out over open-air training and parade grounds. The third precinct, the Spirit, at the uppermost site elevation, includes a healing center, memorial park, water terraces, and an observation tower that overlooks the entire site. Connected by a sequence of six bridges intended to evoke the passage from novice to master, each precinct retains its distinct character within the broader continuity of the constructed landscape.

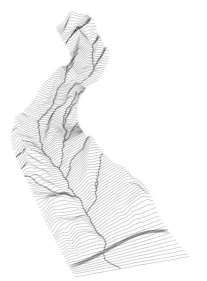

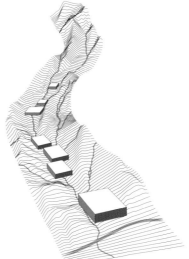

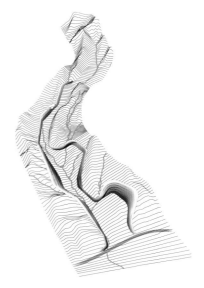

Existing Site
Steep slopes and natural springs define the site.

Dispersed Programs
The competition brief proposed program elements distributed throughout the valley.

Ascending Passages
The master plan fluidly embeds programs within the contours of the topography and allows the free flow of water.

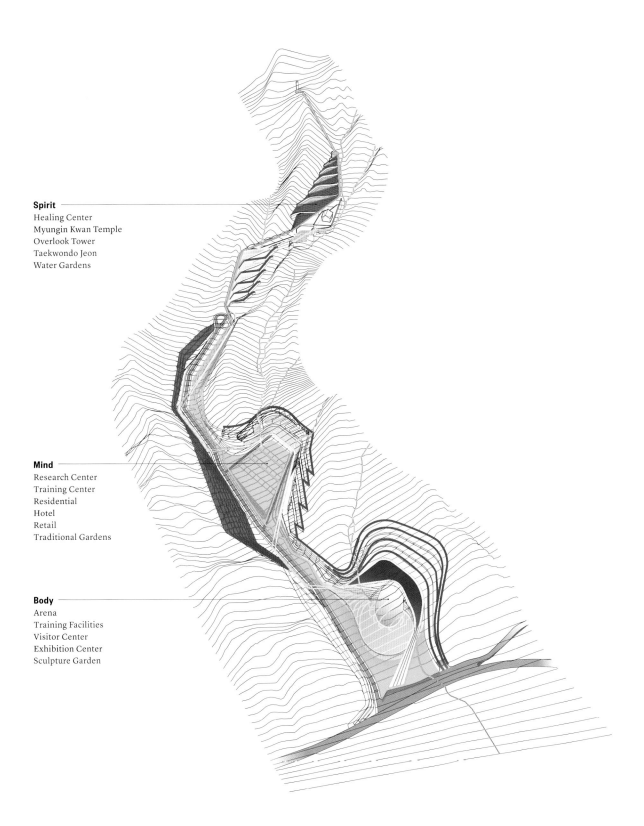

Spirit
Healing Center
Myungin Kwan Temple
Overlook Tower
Taekwondo Jeon
Water Gardens

Mind
Research Center
Training Center
Residential
Hotel
Retail
Traditional Gardens

Body
Arena
Training Facilities
Visitor Center
Exhibition Center
Sculpture Garden

In the choreography of conflict and practice, the discrete components of Taekwondo cannot be considered apart from their relation to one another. When mapped over time, each poomsae, or "form" in Taekwondo, produces a continuous spatial sequence that is part pattern, part sinuous flow. The design of the park embraces Taekwondo's relational topography, complementing the individual precincts with a continuous hydrological band that descends through the valley and a series of water gardens, amplifying both the sustainable and scenic qualities of the site.

Here, sophisticated water management practices promote traditional Korean agriculture on the valley floor, where an abundance of water and nutrients enable the cultivation of traditional crops. The buildings themselves are calibrated to respond to the layered topographies of the site.

The park is organized around three distinct precincts that symbolically represent body, mind, and spirit. The first precinct, the Body, anchors the scheme, and is defined by an iconic arena that creates an active gathering place for visitors.

Each poomsae, or "form" in Taekwondo, produces a continuous spatial sequence that is based on both flow and pattern. The circulation of the master plan is inspired by this network of continuous movements.

TAEGEUK IL JANG
HEAVEN

TAEGEUK YI JANG
LAKE

TAEGEUK SAM JANG
FIRE

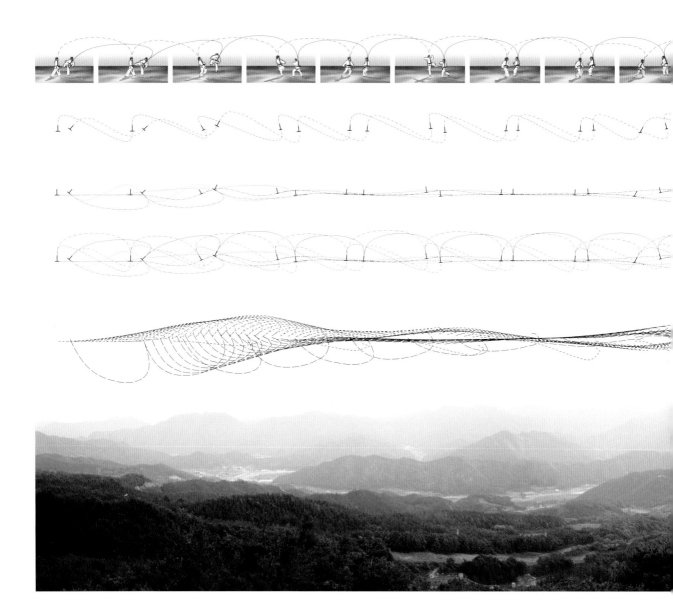

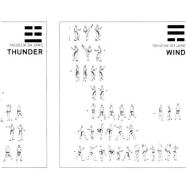

TAEGEUK SA JANG
THUNDER

TAEGEUK OH JANG
WIND

TAEGEUK YOOK JANG
WATER

TAEGEUK CHIL JANG
MOUNTAIN

TAEGEUK SAM JANG
EARTH

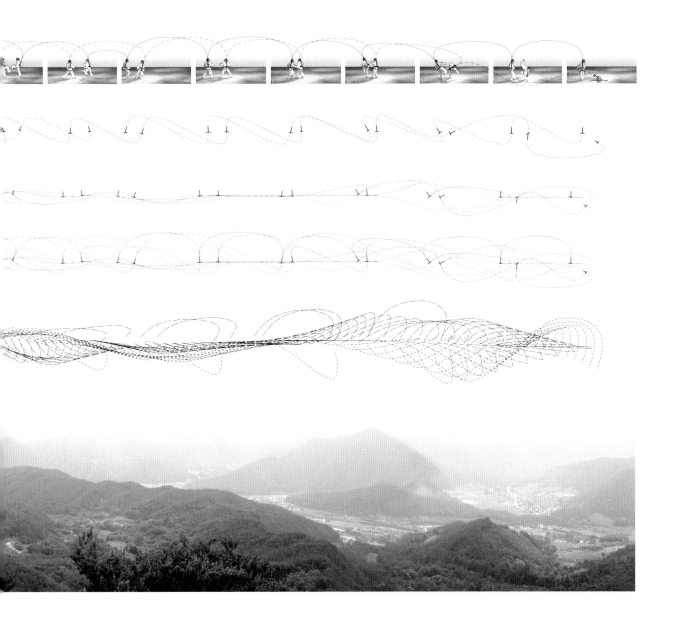

Type A

Type B

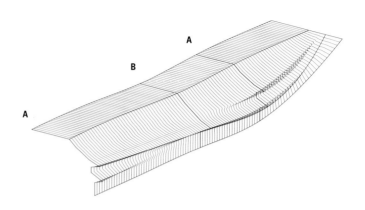

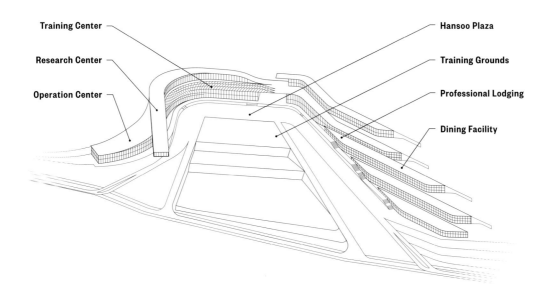

Training Center

Research Center

Operation Center

Hansoo Plaza

Training Grounds

Professional Lodging

Dining Facility

In an effort to cultivate architecture and landscape together, buildings are embedded into the mountainous slopes, limiting interruption of the site's contours and circulation. Recalling the principles of the martial art it supports, the robust yet subtle infrastructure of Taekwondo Park possesses a form of self-sufficiency—a layered destination for events, art, recreation, and renewal—that honors the unique practice and principles of Taekwondo.

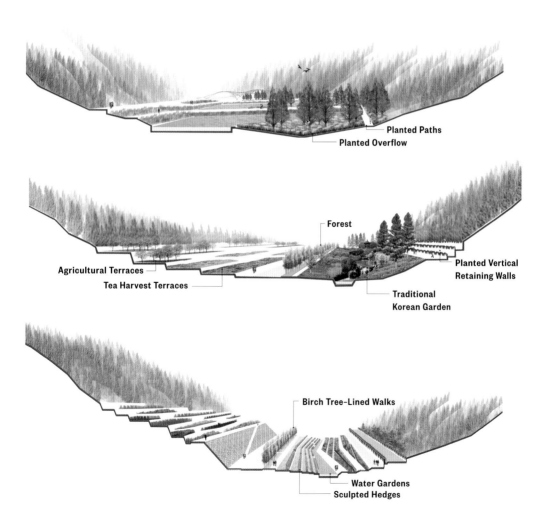

Planted Paths

Planted Overflow

Forest

Agricultural Terraces

Tea Harvest Terraces

Planted Vertical
Retaining Walls

Traditional
Korean Garden

Birch Tree-Lined Walks

Water Gardens
Sculpted Hedges

Brooklyn Botanic Garden Visitor Center

Brooklyn, New York

A botanic garden is an unusual kind of museum—
a fragile collection constantly in flux. As a constructed natural environment composed of a living
collection, such a garden depends on man-made
infrastructures to thrive. Founded in 1910 the
Brooklyn Botanic Garden is an international model
for urban horticulture, hosting illustrative clas-
sical gardens that include the Cherry Esplanade,
Japanese Garden, and Cranford Rose Garden
within its fifty-two acres. Designed by the Olmsted
brothers, Frederick Law Olmsted Jr. and John
Charles Olmsted, on the grounds of a former
coal ash dump, the Botanic Garden now serves as
an oasis within the heart of Brooklyn, visually
separated from the neighborhood by trees and
elevated berms.

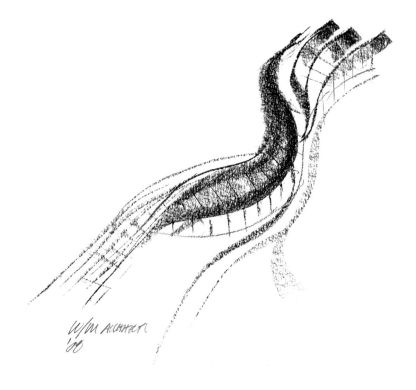

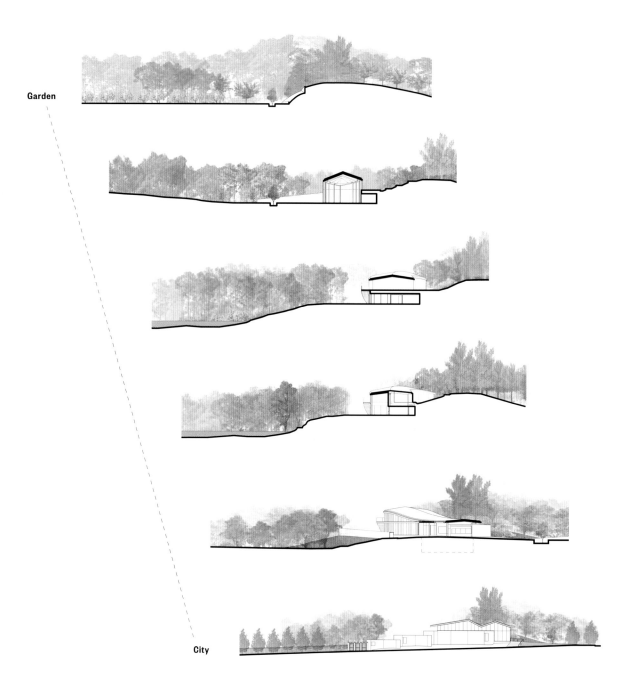

Garden

City

1 Entry Plaza and Ticketing
2 Retail Pavilion
3 Exhibition
4 Event Space
5 Japanese Pond
6 Cherry Walk
7 Ginkgo Allée

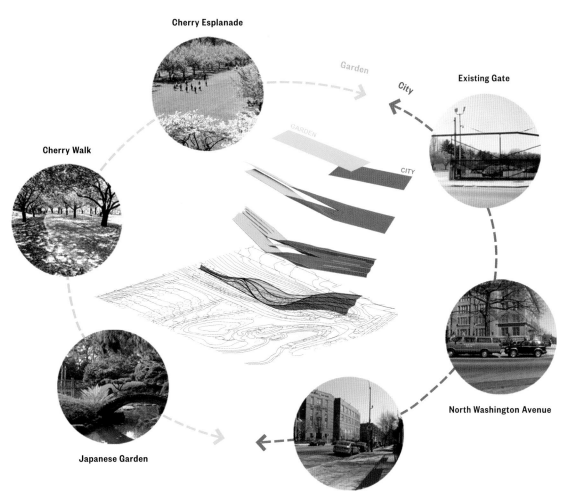

Cherry Esplanade

Garden

City

Existing Gate

GARDEN

CITY

Cherry Walk

North Washington Avenue

Japanese Garden

South Washington Avenue

To provoke curiosity and interest in its world-class collection, the Brooklyn Botanic Garden Visitor Center provides a legible point of arrival and orientation, an interface between garden and city, culture and cultivation. The Visitor Center was conceived as a cinematic threshold that gradually unfolds from an active street-side plaza and garden shop through exhibition galleries to an event space that mediates the transition outdoors to a terraced patio, spilling into the garden beyond. Inspired by the layered and wandering pathways of the historic landscape, a secondary route from atop an embedded berm, which plays host to the garden's scenic Ginkgo Allée, slides through the upper level of the Visitor Center and descends via a grand stair to the main level of the Garden—seamlessly connecting previously disconnected areas of the garden.

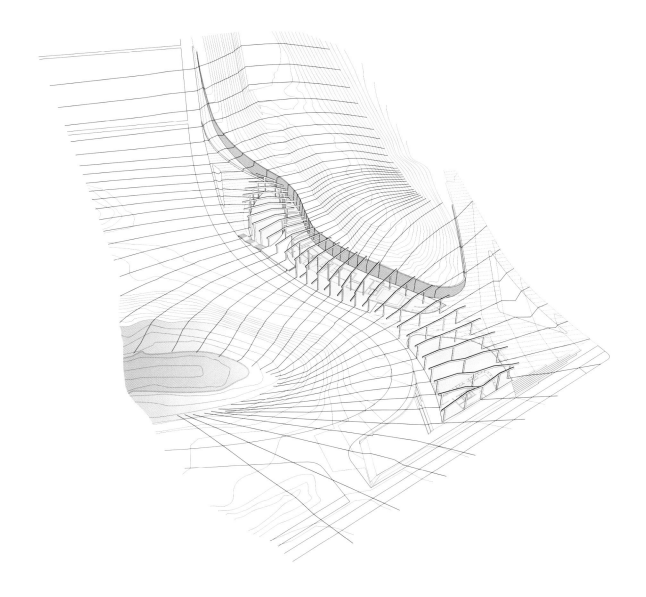

A spiral of movement simultaneously exposes small moments of discovery into and through the building and gardens, while also weaving the building into the earth, acting both as emergent topography and constructed landform. Though experienced from all possible routes as a continuous progression, the twenty-two-thousand-square-foot Visitor Center consists of two structures threaded together by a glazed breezeway that cuts a double curve through the site and unifies the garden's existing pathways. This serpentine route is echoed in the structures themselves, which alternately merge with the undulating topography of the site and break from it to form crystalline pavilion spaces at each end of the circulation spine. The curved, fritted glass walls defining these intimate spaces allow veiled views of the garden across the length of the site, acting as a mediating surface between the building and the landscape.

Like the gardens, the building is experienced cinematically and never seen in its entirety. Garden pathways extend above, around, and through the building—a canopy shelters the main entry route and connects to an upper-level garden.

Sensing the Garden

An elegant, leaf-shaped event
space connects inside and outside,
presenting breathtaking views of
the Cherry Esplanade. A clerestory
level reveals the upper garden and
pathway that slips through the
building. Interior wood paneling is
milled from ginkgo trees that were
harvested from the building site.

Like the garden, the Visitor Center evolves over time. More than a vegetated canopy, the building's ten-thousand-square-foot "living roof" adopts four distinct identities throughout the seasons, providing a new botanical topography of varying heights and colors based on the seasonal life of its plantings. The Visitor Center is a showcase for environmental education—its sustainable features, such as rain gardens, geothermal system, and native plantings, are highlighted throughout the grounds to increase awareness of the use of efficient systems in the public realm. A sustainably rich structure, the Visitor Center redefines the physical and philosophical relationship between visitor and garden, introducing new connections between landscape and structure, exhibition and movement.

A New Green Roof Model
The lush, curving green roof of the Visitor Center will be an ongoing laboratory for the botanic garden and a research tool for the region. This outdoor garden is curated to test an expanded palette of plant species for green roofs in the Northeast. Seen here are research plots prepared by the garden's horticulturalists during the design process.

Terms
and Conditions

Preston Scott Cohen
Felipe Correa
Keller Easterling
Paul Lewis
Hashim Sarkis
Nader Tehrani

Moderated by
Marion Weiss
Michael A. Manfredi
Justin Fowler

Introduction

Marion Weiss | **Michael A. Manfredi** | **Justin Fowler**

The territory of architecture should concern itself with the whole of the built environment. Traditional distinctions—between architecture and landscape, engineering and urbanism, art and ecology—constrain the architectural project and allow architects to sidestep a direct engagement with critical social and environmental issues of our time. Though every project, regardless of scale, is a fertile site for this broader definition of architecture, the largest works of spatial organization are rarely informed by architectural expertise.

There remains, however, a persistent and vital lineage of architectural work animated by big ambitions and innovative takes on the future that cannot simply be ignored. Inspired by the seminal Modernist experiments of figures such as Le Corbusier, Fumihiko Maki, and Paul Rudolph that merged visionary speculation with social, logistical, and technological possibility, our approach is both embedded in and emerging from this layered site.

In considering the evolution of ecological, urban, and social infrastructures, we have been interested in the ambitions and unfulfilled promise of the architectural "mega-project." We believe this legacy of modernism is a project with new potential to act at a scale commensurate with the magnitude and complexity of today's challenges. In analyzing the components, processes, and motivations behind such large-scale works, points of reciprocity between disciplines and scales of operation have illuminated the potential for even the smallest project to serve as a catalyst for urban transformation. Whether the project packages complex internal systems in an iconic form that mediates between the demands of a specialized program and campus such as the Krishna P. Singh Center for Nanotechnology at University of Pennsylvania, or merges the complexities of architectural demands within the topographic identity of a city such as our projects for the Seattle Art Museum and Brooklyn Botanic Garden, the conventions of architecture have altered the evolution of their site's infrastructure.

Discourses on the mega-project are often vague and serve as an umbrella for an uneasy alliance of potentially divergent approaches to large-scale intervention in the built environment. With these preoccupations in mind, we initiated a conversation with colleagues to reconsider the legacy and promise of the mega-project. The following discourse presents a conversation of past and present—a cross-section of mega-projects in history, both built and unbuilt, supported with provisional definitions of key terminology, excerpts from historical texts, and selections from our conversations with contemporary practitioners and scholars, providing a running commentary that begins to put forward a more precise language by which to engage the forms and infrastructural ambitions of the "mega-."

Intended as a grammar of approaches and attributes, rather than a typological catalog or operational toolkit, this document will give shape to what has largely existed up to this point as attitude, articulating an evolution in the linked practices of infrastructure and urban form.

Form

**Scale | Composition | Arrangement |
Image | Grounding**

Scale

**Measure and proportionality. Often a question of
perspective, a project's scale cannot be evaluated
apart from its physical and sociomaterial contexts.
Today's built mega-projects may put past visions
to shame, yet localized concentrations of effort can
exert large-scale spheres of influence that render
totalizing schemes obsolete.**

Nader Tehrani: It's important not to confuse megaform with the
mega-commission. Mega-projects invariably happen regardless of
whether or not they are critically assessed or somehow conceptualized as megaforms. So many of the projects that are going forward
right now in the rapidly developing world exist at the mega-scale
largely because economies of scale allow for the mobilization
of construction resources, human power, and development all
at the same time. In many respects, the mega-project is a de facto
condition and the majority of that is neither architecture, nor
critical, but always relevant because it does challenge the existing
city, and not necessarily in positive ways.

We also need to recognize that the polemics of the megastructure of the 1950s and 1960s may have been after a structural
synthesis and an overarching organic order that is miniature
in comparison to the mega-economies that control today's landscapes. This scalar difference already sets up a social and economic

Rockefeller Center, by Raymond
Hood, Wallace K. Harrison, and
Max Abramovitz, New York, 1939

Josep Lluís Sert: I think we are suffering
from something today—it's extremes. We
lost something that was very beautiful in
environments, in life in general; there was a
certain balance. For me, "balance" is a word
I've thought about carefully. It's a matter of
scale, a matter of putting certain things near
other things that would have a relationship.
That has been lost—a matter of measure. In
the cities the great loss in applying modern
technology—whatever admirable things
the skyscraper had—is that it hasn't
fit into the infrastructure....I know that
we've invented many things—we have
extraordinary expressways and we have
many things—but these things have never
come together. The expressways and the
skyscrapers aren't related.[1] (1980)

comparison that frames how big has become small over the last fifty years and how the scale of control has also changed. Consider the planning of the Berlin Free University as compared to a big mall project happening somewhere in China today. The Berlin Free University came replete with a structural, mechanical, and planometric syntax that was offered as a kind of architectural investment. Although the mall in China is not lacking architecture, it is probably being parceled off into dozens of buildings to be managed by many architects, all taking charge of a fragmented labor force themed around different economic agendas and planning strategies that are subdivisible and somehow depleting the power of the singular.

Paul Lewis: I think megaform does exist and is operative, but it comes from the scaling up of a building type and it maintains its autonomy whether it's in the form of a super large stadium or a shopping mall. The megastructure seems to operate less through its own autonomy and much more in terms of its horizontal integration with the city. It lacks an individual identity. You could refer to an entire city as a megastructure. As an individual architect, you don't tend to get RFPs to do megastructures, whereas megaforms can be the product of a particular approach to a project. Of course, being operative in terms of practice is very different from being conceptually interesting.

Kenneth Frampton: Architecture is not big sculpture.[2] (2011)

Preston Scott Cohen: It's crucial to note that "mega-" takes on a different meaning when you're referring to architecture as opposed to urbanism. Rockefeller Center is the eruption of a miniature pattern within the larger scheme of the grid. It's actually a smaller-scale development in the context of the city's block structure, but it exists at the scale of architecture. By virtue of taking over a territory greater than buildings normally do, it develops urbanity within itself that is at the architectural scale. I'm very interested in this inverse relationship, where architecture has to be a small city to be a mega-scaled project. Mega-urbanism is something else entirely.

Felipe Correa: Issues of continuity in the city need to be put against their limitations. Things work at certain scales but stop working when you shift to another. The idea of the continuous surface, which has been exhaustively played out recently, has to be tested against that. Property ownership has a certain set of domains. There are certain systems in the city that are continuous and certain systems that are discontinuous. I think the idea of the continuous surface, or of the megaform, is only valid when it proposes an intelligent alternative to the canons of continuity and discontinuity already established by the context.

Arthur Drexler: Is it possible that our buildings, far from being too big, are really not big enough?[3] (1967)

Hashim Sarkis: Both megastructure and megaform share one obvious attribute. They are mega. But they are mega in terms of their impact, not necessarily their size. Sometimes size is important, but not always. An impact on the city through the skyline—through the silhouette—does not require as much size as strategic location. Another thing they share is the idea that architecture has a responsibility toward the order of the larger environment. The main difference, as I understand it, is that the megastructure is partly infrastructural in its behavior. It is meant to make its impact by affecting the performance of the systems it plugs into. The megaform depends primarily on the visceral response to its scale and presence.

Composition

Figuration and part-to-whole relationships. Generated from intuitive or systemic processes, compositional logics can range from the continuous to the discrete. These logics cut across scales and inform choices about a project's necessary level of architectonic articulation.

Reyner Banham: Grand Central Station… emphatically does not look like a megastructure, but its vast and multi-functional ramifications can be experienced as one and it is organized as one.[4] (1976)

Paul Lewis: Considered in light of architecture's obsession with the idea of continuity, Grand Central Station is interesting in that it's a phenomenal sectional engine imaged as a very clear object. The envelope is able to suspend the station's operational qualities quite effectively. What appears to be a linear, one-dimensional system becomes quite thick in a very interesting way. That sectional move is not at all legible on the outside of the building. All of the issues of incline, which ultimately are connected to some idea of instability, movement, and flux, are countered by the imagery of the building. It's a building that's doing everything it can to hide or masquerade its inner sensibility. The Beaux-Arts diagrams were not about articulating the section, they were about how you coordinate a plan and then place a facade on the plan. The program of Grand Central forced the architects to include things that were not part of the architectural repertoire and they had to find a way to bury them and still do an architectural project, whereas now, everyone wants to image the section as the building.

Nader Tehrani: "Continuity" may very well be the single most abused term of the last fifteen years, but it's also an important one. It has

been used both literally and rhetorically. On the one hand, it has
had a basic urbanistic motivation, linking surfaces, extending the
ground, creating connections between the inside and the outside.
On the other hand, its rhetorical use has been exercised in a variety
of projects in the hands of Neil Denari, Diller Scofidio + Renfro,
the Office for Metropolitan Architecture (OMA), and Foreign
Office Architects, among others, adopting extended surfaces that
symbolically produce continuities that are never intended to be
navigated—linking floors, walls, and ceilings in single swoops, and

Grand Central Station, by Reed
and Stem, Warren and Wetmore,
New York, 1913

essentially functioning as a representational device for the continuity or fluidity of capital, networks, and other such characteristic
phenomena identified from our times. Such symbolic continuity is
meant to suggest that, precisely because social, political, economic,
and material territories need to be divided and need separation, we
require a symbolic form that makes something larger than what the
various constituencies can tolerate in their actual programmatic
requirements and adjacencies.

Paul Lewis: Any ramp that provides three feet of continuity provides
some fifty feet of discontinuity along its edges. I'm less interested
in the legibility of continuity in the form of image, but instead about
how the form works and if it is able to dissolve its discontinuity or
deal with it in a successful way. Compare Wright's treatment of the
circulation in the Guggenheim, where he turns the edge discontinuity of that ramp into an atrium in order to make it disappear, to
someone like Koolhaas, who, in any number of his projects, seeks
to intensify the discontinuity. He's interested in absolute incompatibility and friction along those edges.

Felipe Correa: In either case, a megaform or a megastructure requires
a continuous formal identity. At the end of the day there's something
that ties it together that goes beyond just spatial continuity. A
master plan might be made up of discrete pieces that make a larger
block, but for a megaform or a megastructure, its base infrastructure
is always continuous and its components share a common language.
Rockefeller Center is a fantastic mega-project that cannot easily be

Vincent Scully: Compressed to slab form, they also became essentially space-definers rather than mid-space elements, and it was as such that they formed what can still properly be called the finest spatial grouping of skyscrapers the world has seen: Rockefeller Center. In the deserved praise which Rockefeller Center has received, it has all too seldom been pointed out that the arrangement is pure Beaux-Arts, a little stolid perhaps, but axial, focused, and firm, shaping a shopping street with places to sit and a small square in which it is possible to do something or to watch people doing things. The huge vertical slabs dramatize that space and those actions, and the single basic alteration which the architects made in the first design succeeded in bringing them all to life: one slab was turned at right angles to the major axis, and so set the whole group in pinwheeling motion but left the central space axially defined.[5] (1969)

classified according to the categories of megaform or megastructure. In plan, it acts as a traditional urban project, but in section it takes on the characteristics of a megastructure through a thickened base that unifies its collection of vertical pieces. It manages to respect the structural block and the street grid of Manhattan while maintaining a continuous material palette throughout its entirety. It holds a particular identity that makes it distinct from the rest of the city, and its singularity is the means by which it engenders a transformation of the urban fabric.

Guggenheim Museum, by
Frank Lloyd Wright, New York,
1959

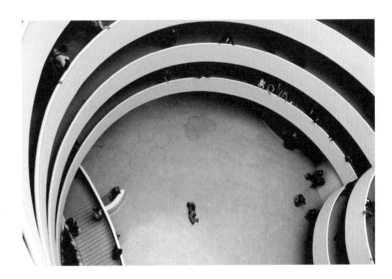

Drawing of Raymond Hood,
Wallace K. Harrison, and
Max Abramovitz's Rockefeller
Center, by Ceri Edmunds, 2011

Arrangement

Configuration and spatial organization. Arrangement strategies can work with, against, or in parallel to compositional logics. Modular aggregations or serial assemblages can be deployed in the formation of a coherent figure, but can just as well act to confound singular readings of a project.

Sigfried Giedion: All urban planning must become dynamic in consequence of this unprecedented flood of population to the metropolitan cities…It is now clear to everyone that this unparalleled population growth and the traffic chaos within the city organism indicate a completely different way of life and demand radical changes.

Proposals to handle the situation pile up endlessly—cities under the ground, cities hovering above the ground on steel scaffolding—proposals that would schematize the complex organism of the city more drastically even than the traditional two-dimensional checkerboard pattern. What is needed is a completely new attitude toward the structure of the city. The contemporary planner must be fully aware that he must simultaneously satisfy the most heterogeneous needs and create a "dynamic field" in which these forces are related to one another. In place of the rigid master plan proposed in the early years of the century a flexible "master program" is now being put forward, one that allows for changes and that leaves open-ended possibilities for the future. An example is the plan for the Free University in West Berlin by Candilis, Josic, and Woods, which creates only a framework and everywhere leaves openings for future developments.[6] (1967)

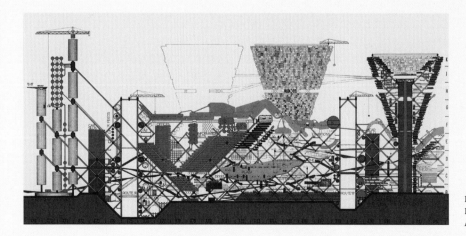

Plug-In City, Section,
Max Pressure Area, by Peter Cook,
Archigram, 1964

Master Plan for Almere,
by OMA, Almere, 2007

Keller Easterling: There seems to be something in the air with so many large-scale projects creeping away from any kind of structure that could be considered to be a single building, which we would evaluate by profile and shape. There is something else going on that exceeds the notion of a traditional building type. So many of the postwar megastructures were serial assemblages. The virtue of a serial approach meant that you could add one more piece to the whole or three more and it would remain iconic without resolving into a single, finite piece. That's an aspect of the megastructure that lends itself to an alternative notion of form-making. It's characterized by a certain unboundedness that might allow for the migration of pieces to wherever they're magnetized within an area that would only loosely be called a site. The strength of such forms breaks down, however, in the instances where their repetition is softened through the introduction of a continuous landscape or a unifying gestural thread.

Felipe Correa: There are moments where systematic repetition is necessary to accommodate multiple hands, but they have to be very clearly defined. A megaform as an objectified piece in the landscape can allow you to define and synthesize particular portions of a project that require a level of specificity or definition to be able to engage with its context, to be able to actually meet the street. In my own work, I'm constantly dealing with this negotiation between the systematic repetition of architectural elements and the more

Foreign Office Architects: As opposed to the assemblage between structure and circulation, which blended in a metamorphic manner, the program [for the Yokohama Port Terminal] was to become integrated in a more sedimentary form. The programmatic strategies used in the project can be related to an interest in exploring what we would roughly denominate as intensive space: that is, the kind of spatiality where the capacity of space is not directly related to its size, and where the quality of space varies differentially, rather than as a discontinuity.[7] (2003)

Analysis of Yokohama Port
Terminal, by Pablo Roquero,
2011

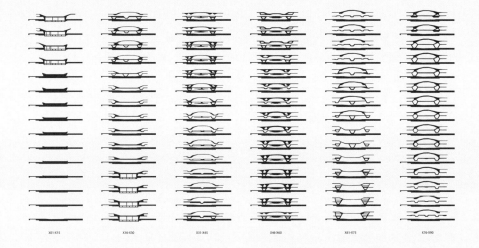

Yokohama Port Terminal,
by Foreign Office of Architects,
Tokyo, 2002

synthetic resolution of the section. The recognition of this interplay is a very important design tool when thinking at a larger scale.

For all their differences, both megaform and megastructure rely on the presence of architecture in the city. They're not the city, but they are a fragment of the city that is transformed through architecture. That's also what distinguishes them from the concept of a master plan. OMA's project for Almere is an interesting model because it combines a very particular sort of megastructure that then is accommodated by a larger urban project—a larger grid—that becomes an extension of the town.

Nader Tehrani: Villa Moda, our project for Kuwait City, is perhaps a good example of a megaform because it does touch on the dichotomy of the literal and the symbolic. To contextualize that project, we were given a mission by the client to occupy a variety of parcels of land in segregated ways, as an office park, mall, arena, and hotel; all of them as separate entities fenced off from each other, the sum total of which was to create a new economic engine for the sixth ring road of Kuwait City. Housing was absent from the program. The first thing we suggested was to avoid segregating the project into six different parcels, proposing instead to make it one project so as to become the beginnings of a city. In other words, if we produce an integrated series of programmatic overlaps they will have the power economically and physically to sponsor more activity and actually grow out of that. And secondly, we said that if you cap off the entire project with housing, what you offer is a twenty-four-hour presence that will produce another populating economy so that it's not merely a destination for shopping, but is actually a generator for a center of occupation from which people travel out of as much as into. In that sense, the structural continuity of the "megastructural" ceiling is both literal and symbolic. It's a reflected ceiling plan project. In a project that has no facade, the reflected ceiling plan is both the facade and the symbolic presence of the building. More than that, however, an environment with such brutal heat necessitates the shade and environmental engineering offered by the continuous ceiling, which promises a certain perfor- mance that extends the winter by one month in both directions. Finally, the geometric calisthenics we undertook to reconcile the

Villa Moda, by Office dA, 2007

typological differences of the spaces underneath—between, say, round arenas, square souks, and triangulated auditoriums—are really architectural specifications that are dealing with the problem of how to express continuity where it really counts. For the Kuwait project this problem was in reconciling all of those differences in a piece of infrastructure that is at once structural but also geometrically aligned with those things that need to be different—both in terms of form and performance.

Paul Rudolph: The Ponte Vecchio—the shops along the pedestrian way, and over it the marvellous housing. The scale of supports is in keeping with the vehicular way, and then there is a working down of scale. There is nothing new. That is a megastructure, and probably the purest example in traditional architecture.[8] (1976)

Felipe Correa: The issue of formal articulation in the infrastructural mega-project has to do with asking certain questions that cannot be answered through programmatic juxtaposition or through the literal juxtaposition of different speeds in the city. Many of the questions that have to do with the articulation of different systems

Diagrams of Compositional Form, Megaform, and Group Form, from *Investigations in Collective Form*, by Fumihiko Maki, 1964

and different components of the city have to be resolved formally. What's ultimately going to determine the success of a project is the way that you shape those spaces and calibrate those adjacencies. It has less to do with the number of programs or intermodalities you can stuff into a single package and more with trying to identify the most appropriate set of forms that can actually establish the relationships you want. The formal answers might not emerge from the program of the systems themselves, but will come through an interrogation of the physical and experiential identities of the site through the disciplinary lens of architecture.

Keller Easterling: I'm drawn to forms like that of Olmsted's Emerald Necklace because the path it goes along is not as important as the interdependent protocols governing its structure. That's also why I like Benton MacKaye. With the Appalachian Trail, he essentially wasn't designing anything but a footpath and a specific set of parameters for how it could be traveled. But he didn't know what the final shape would be, even if it was the product of a very explicit design. Some of the projects in Weiss/Manfredi's studio at the Harvard GSD also relied on a limited formal repertoire that could be deployed systemically to colonize the site.

Emerald Necklace, by Frederick Law Olmsted, Boston, 1894

Image

Shape, silhouette, and gestalt. Largely inseparable from symbolic content, a project's image can take on the abstraction of a contour or the short-cut precision of a logo. Most often associated with issues of legibility or iconicity, image is also commonly evoked as a form of context critique, where the incoherent visual noise of an urban site is posited as a condition in need of an architectural remedy.

Reyner Banham: A megastructure was also a building which looked like a megastructure.[9] (1976)

Drawing of Le Corbusier's Plan Obus for Algiers, by Alexandria Lee, 2011

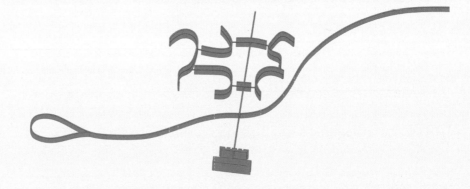

Le Corbusier: The straight line is deeply impressive in the confusion of nature; it is the work of men. It is inspiring and even poetical in the midst of this nondescript landscape.... Look at the railway; it goes straight on, conscious of its job; it is a witness to human will—a positive thing.[10] (1929)

Keller Easterling: Projects that deliberately make a very specific geometric profile choose to exercise the power of a stone in the water.

Paul Lewis: We don't have a lot of tools to use as architects even if we think we do. There is almost always some obligation to image as a means to test a project. For better or worse, the projection of a possible future through models and perspectives is much more seductive than a diagram of possible scenarios that lends itself to metrics. The image of a particular project might get in the way of a more intricate unfolding of that project. There's a friction, for example, between a master plan and the individual buildings in that master plan. A master plan tends to be accompanied by a photoshopped view of the planner's vision for the developed outcome of the plan, and more often than not that view is at odds with some of the possibilities that could come out of that same plan. It is a pedagogical issue as well, because within the context of a semester-long design studio you can't test a work except through some form of image, even if it might be at odds with the more intriguing, less optical ambitions of the project.

Nader Tehrani: The silhouette relates directly to the question of rhetoric. There are certain instances where differences have to be sustained for basic practical reasons, and so without the rhetoric of continuity those differences could not be concealed. Other times, particularly in the current era, notions of form and performance have been brought into alignment precisely to produce a more evocative alibi for continuity. FOA's project in Yokohama is an example of that, where the development of ramps and inhabitable surfaces becomes a vehicle by which to convey an image of inevitability. It has a silhouette on the skyline, but it is actually composed of markings on the ground in plan and section that are the manifestation of codes. The code of a ramp and stair vary, and the project goes from the flat to the sloped to the stair in various iterations, essentially indexing the possibility of continuity both in its smoothness and its less-than-smooth conditions. A range of other projects situate themselves between these two extremes. It's about taking the most salient parameters—whether they're cultural or formal—and hyperbolizing them until they become the architectural signifier.

Habitat 67 logo, by Moshe Safdie,
Montreal, 1967

Paul Lewis: It's almost impossible in my mind to design a megaform without being intentionally and optimistically naïve. The level of complexity involves a huge investment of time. With extremely large urban projects not only do you have a kind of incompatibility between the ability to design and implement, but such a project tends to fall prey to the fact that it can't be designed without the accumulation of time. As students of architecture we take great pleasure in the amazing ambitions of the mega-projects of the twentieth century, but their failures serve as such a cautionary tale that it killed our curiosity and ambition.

Keller Easterling: A building like the Free University in Berlin is still so beholden to a tradition of visual composition. That's its limit. It's funny that we're actually satisfied with the limits often imposed on object form.

Habitat 67, 1967

Paul Lewis: What is produced from the logo of a shape beyond a certain commercial or iconic value? I'm seduced by Bob Somol's arguments about shape and its effects, as it's intriguing to consider how an emphasis on shape starts to provide certain degrees of freedom for architectural articulation. But we need further thinking and experimentation with the efficacy of shape, so that it's not simply reduced to an issue of logo.

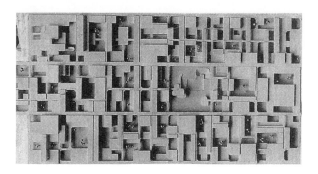

My issue with the "shape" project and even with certain autonomous manifestations of the megaform is that they typically operate as impositions and require—rhetorically, if not physically —a blank site. To me, this task is more about how you evolve, accumulate, and intensify existing conditions.

Berlin Free University Model, by Candilis-Josic-Woods, Berlin, 1963

Grounding

Topographic orientation. Bound both by the dictates of site and the possibilities of imaging, a project's grounding can imply either a tailored fit or a casual skirting of the landscape. Grounding is also greatly informed by representation with the figure-ground plan, the continuous section, and the three-dimensional rendering, each suggesting a different aesthetic and spatial function.

Fumihiko Maki: The megastructure is a large frame in which all the functions of a city or part of a city are housed. It has been made possible by present day technology. In a sense, it is a man-made feature of the landscape. It is like the great hill on which Italian hill towns were built.[11] (1964)

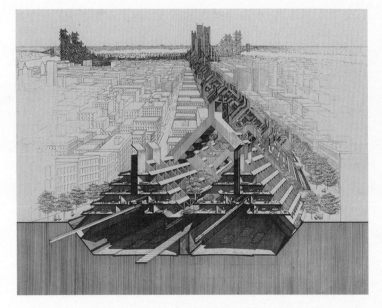

Drawing of Lower Manhattan Expressway, by Paul Rudolph, 1967

Preston Scott Cohen: You could almost apply the megaform discussion to New York's Murray Hill as much as you could to Rockefeller Center. In the Murray Hill development, there's a moment where the ground plane rises up and suddenly you find yourself—though within the grid system of the city—in a very different context. It doesn't entirely conform to the means by which the primary system defines itself, but it's seamlessly merged with that system. You don't have, as you do with Rockefeller Center, the evidence of singularity as a megaform. No one would call Murray Hill a megaform, but it has one of those essential aspects, which is the deviation from the ground. It's a landform. It acts as if it is going to participate in what exists, but actually, we discover that it's not the same.

Carpenter Center, by
Le Corbusier, Cambridge,
Massachusetts, 1963

Kenneth Frampton: While the megaform may display certain megastructural characteristics, the large scale manifestation and expression of its intrinsic structure is not its primary significance. What is much more pertinent in the case of the megaform is the topographic, horizontal thrust of the overall profile together with the programmatic place-creating character of its intrinsic program.[12] (2010)

Preston Scott Cohen: I don't think Koolhaas actually wants to be part of the participatory tradition embodied by Rockefeller Center. By making his buildings truly different through and through, while writing that he believes that the city has already generated the kind of potential that architecture can have, implies that he thinks it could be a source for the regeneration of the city and that's a kind

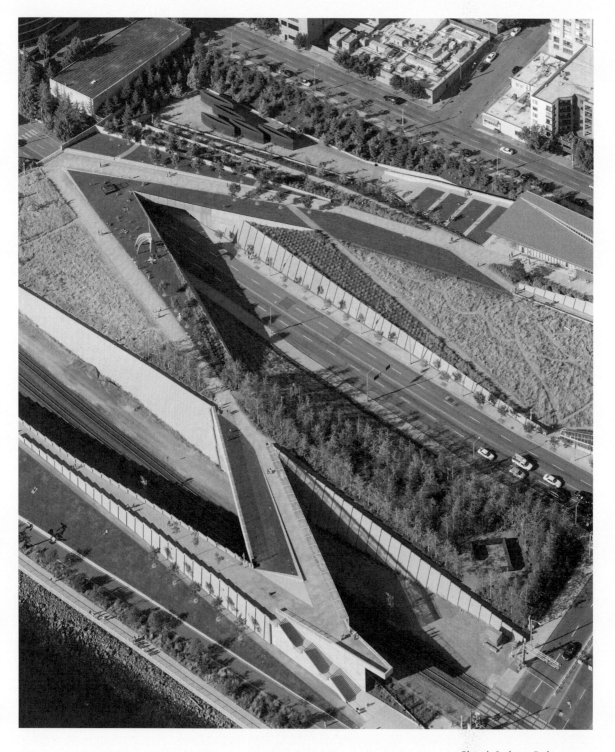

Olympic Sculpture Park,
by Weiss/Manfredi, Seattle, 2007

of utopian ambition. If he were to merge or dissolve himself and the boundaries of his work, it would accept too much as given. I'm more sympathetic to the idea of not being able to see where one thing leaves off and another begins. In some ways, that's an Eisenmanian way of treating the city. The Wexner Center is not at all dissimilar from Le Corbusier's Carpenter Center, which acts by pulling the sidewalks of the system of the campus and morphing them into something else. The Olympic Sculpture Park in Seattle is another work that operates in this way. In these cases, I don't think you would know that you were in the territory of an authored work until after a certain point, but you couldn't identify precisely when that moment occurs. The interplay or recalibration between attention and distraction produces an effect that challenges our conscious recognition. I'm interested in the process of morphing; of montage, rather than collage. Koolhaas's work belongs to this latter idea. It's about contesting or foiling. His work definitely presents a figure against the ground. Inclusivity and exclusivity are two very different modes of thought.

Position

Inclusion | Lamination | Economy | Proliferation | Utopia

Inclusion

Physical and conceptual domains. Public and private, architecture and urbanism, author and collective; each pair conjures a relation between distinct domains or disciplines, instantiating their separation while simultaneously blurring their boundaries. The contemporary mega-project is a manifestation of these seemingly paradoxical oscillations.

Euralille Master Plan,
by OMA, Lille, France, 1994

Felipe Correa: Beyond being an issue of formal articulation, I think the difference between a megaform and megastructure has to do with how flexible the formal system is in accommodating multiple hands or authors over time. The megaform tends to be authored by a single individual (or team), because its structure is not organized in a schematic way that can accommodate a multiplicity of hands as a project evolves over time. The megastructure is much more systemic and allows for such evolutionary collaboration. Compare, for example, the Arnhem Train Station by UN Studio to a project such as Euralille by OMA. Arnhem has a complex infrastructural base with a series of towers on top, but at the end of the day a single office or a single author has to conceptualize the megaform of the base and the towers for it to make sense as a project. With Euralille, even though it's not a completely repetitive structure it responds more to the idea of a megastructure in that there's an underlying infrastructural piece that allows for multiple authors and multiple hands to be able to build it over time. The question then turns to the range of control between the larger morphology and the author-ship of the individual pieces. Some of the most successful projects are the ones that calibrate this tension well and understand that a successful urban morphology or urban project doesn't necessarily guarantee successful architecture.

Preston Scott Cohen: The boundary between architecture and urbanism is essentially a question about authorship. The moment at which you begin to modify the underlying system that gives rise to the order of buildings in the city, you're making a distinction that defines it as authored. And further, with the avant garde's move toward the dissolution of the author, the question would be: could the city replace the tradition of the architecture as the progenitor of forms and social organizations? Will the city usurp architecture's role in defining the utopian? Koolhaas saw it in Manhattan retroac-tively. It didn't need a manifesto to project into the future because it was unconsciously there all along and architecture could never do as much as the city could do. Rem heralded the supremacy of urbanism. I argue that what he does is pretend that his buildings are an extension of the existing city, but the ruse and the conceit always makes his buildings utterly distinct from the forms of the normal patterns. I didn't think, for example, that CCTV was a major building of Rem's until recently when I saw the structural model. The building is filled with structure. It is so omnipresent, but in a new formation; not the forms we take for granted. He's making the mega-system evident by changing its form so radically.

CCTV Headquarters, by OMA, Beijing, 2012

Hashim Sarkis: Importantly, the megastructure/megaform debate takes us back to a moment in history (is it a real moment?) when we did not have that disciplinary and professional distinction between architecture and urbanism or between landscape and architecture, when it was all Architecture with a big "A." (This is different from, but not opposed to, Scott Cohen's "capital 'A' architecture.") Faced with the responsibility of addressing the public role of architecture, the distinctions between media and forms versus systems, plants and water versus brick and pavement, degrees of authorship, etc., are reduced to trivial Byzantinisms. This moment may be hypothetical but it does precede several real moments or attempts at overemphasizing the boundary between architecture and urbanism: Christopher Alexander's insistence that the teapot cannot be designed with the same methods as the city, or the different receptions of Koolhaas' tropes, from delirium to bigness, where the responsibility toward the public is generally confounded with that toward the city.

Paul Lewis: I'm more and more convinced that what we're going to be doing as architects is the tactical and strategic modification of existing structures through wit, cleverness, specificity of material use, programming, etc. Building from the ground up will become less and less relevant.

Preston Scott Cohen: The mega-scale forces us to evaluate the distinction between private and public, particularly as it relates to the interior. Would it be fair to say that encapsulated space or junkspace is closer to architecture than to urbanism because the management or disciplining of the space is more clearly under a single authority? Is that a megaform? It is infrastructure, certainly. Architecture has always had as one of its primary tasks the need to define the relation between the individual and the collective. We have to theorize the difference between being in a city when there's no thermal distinction between the signature vendors and the common area of a mall in all those "interiorized," encapsulated urbanisms like Atlanta, Minneapolis, and Houston, as opposed to the thermal barrier being one of the means by which you recognize the boundary that separates the discrete building from the city as an integrated system. Even outdoor spaces have their public and private areas, but the distinction is exacerbated and formalized so radically by the thermal barrier that such a boundary is fundamental. Playing with that limit is perhaps another way to manipulate the dialectic between attention and distraction.

Lamination

Modes of framing and redundancy. Urbanity rarely lends itself to resolution. Development often proceeds through fragments and layers, incomplete projects and unintentional disruptions. Such limits can be recast as generative components for provisional interventions.

Paul Lewis: With our project for MoMA's Rising Currents exhibition, Water Proving Ground, our reference point wasn't a grid or the city, it was an uninhabited flat brownfield the scale of New York's Central Park. And, in some respects, the entire operation of our project was manifest in the slight inclination of topography. So, as opposed to a more complex intersection of building, ground, sidewalk, and city, etc., we really had a very simple thing to negotiate, namely the fluctuations of water and how that shift in section dramatically modified the plan. Everything else was something of an overlay onto that operation. In my mind the project was more a collection of parts than an effective totality. We called those parts "petri dishes," and they were adjacent inclines that could each take on a degree of autonomy. We never saw it operating as a self-contained entity. This approach to the section was then animated with a somewhat fanciful layer of activities and programs to produce a legible project appropriate for the exhibition at MoMA. The need for legible image in the representation placed a limitation on the amount of friction in the project and forced us to collapse the passage of time into a single synthetic moment.

Preston Scott Cohen: I've been riding my bike through New York quite a bit lately, and the city is very different from what it was when I used to live here. This new system of parks and bike lanes is not architecture with a capital "A," but in some sense it's an accidental

architecture. The new city is right on top of the old one and there's
no mutuality, just opposing things. It's not intended, but it does
act as a kind of foil as Rem might want. Being on a bicycle in one
of those new painted bike lanes, I have a very different experience
of the city. When I see people walking, it's like they belong to the
city as it was thirty years ago, and while biking, I'm in this other
thing. It's as if two times collapsed. The pedestrians and cars were
then, I am now, and these parallel systems are not really working
together just yet. At the same time, it helps if the normative patterns
are clearly delineated; in this case, most people in Midtown have
to be walking in order to produce the uncanny experience of being
on the bike. The obsession with the "mega-" is a more disciplinary
version of this phenomenon, where we are set apart from, or set
aside from, the normative condition of the city, and I think now
we are witnessing the products of an archaeological sensibility or
rather the lamination of different systems. We're manifesting a new
system of living onto the old one and that offers a new potential
for people to participate in this other city. People are re-inventing
themselves.

Water Proving Ground, by LTL
Architects, MoMA Rising Currents
exhibition, 2010

Yan'an Elevated Road,
Shanghai, 1996

Felipe Correa: The trans-scalar nature of a project has to do with its ability to create moments in the city where these multiple scales can come together successfully. That's why the idea of the intermodal hub has become so prominent in recent years. There are other ways that go beyond utilitarian purposes that can begin to represent this shift in scale in the way that people experience the city. In recent years, for example, we have seen enormous amounts of money invested in sinking highways, whereas I think you can actually argue that highways are vital parts of cities and can develop urban projects that establish a better dialogue with the highway. One, you would save a lot of money, and two, you would begin to allow for other spaces of representation in the city to come to the forefront, while taking away some of the negative aspects of those projects.

There's also the example of Shanghai, which is a mess in many ways, but something they did very well was to build tall freeways. Even though the cost of elevating them to twice the average height is astronomical, it allowed them to create a particular canopy over the city that shelters an incredible quality of open space underneath. And, while the highway system is extremely efficient and responds to the transportation needs of the city, the fact that it was not conceived entirely around vehicular transportation allowed for the emergence of an experiential identity that becomes complementary to the infrastructure itself.

Economy

Less and more. Economic approaches to the built environment assume a variety of forms. Projects may be conceived on the deployment of an intelligently designed base unit, a careful leveraging of site conditions, or through a creative approach to the political economy of the building process itself.

Reyner Banham: The result (as at Habitat, Montreal) is really a monolithic statue commemorating an ideal of adaptability that was practically impossible to realize in built fact.[13] (1976)

Habitable Bridge,
by Hugh Ferriss, 1920

Nader Tehrani: With Safdie's Habitat, what we learned was that modularity itself was a utopian proposition. When they came to produce modularity, they only ended up with variations of it, and now we have a similar problem with mass customization. We want to be able to make things infinitely flexible and we end up in modularity. At the same time, one also has to consider local material economies and labor costs, which, ironically, might allow for the tackling of custom projects through the brute application of manpower in order to avoid the shipping costs associated with prefabricated elements. Part of the smartness of these modular projects, if you want to take them seriously, is the way in which they're able to leverage the universal aspirations of construction with the local suppleness of mobilizing certain forces to produce innovative things.

Jürgen Joedicke: Candilis-Josic-Woods have never planned for an ideal world, but always in response to definite and distinct demands and needs....Their attitude is founded on the tradition of an uncompromising functionalism, in which the latter is regarded as a method of working and not as a formal characteristic.[14] (1968)

Felipe Correa: It's crucial to begin to rethink the presence of infrastructure, primarily heavyweight mobility infrastructure and its relation to the city. The shift that we've seen in the last ten to fifteen years is that of moving from the postwar idea of infrastructures as singular systems—highways are only highways, they move cars; railroads are only railroads and they move trains—into new complex or hybrid infrastructures that resolve multiple things with a single move. The idea is that the transformation of infrastructure and the development of an urban project can actually be conceived simultaneously instead of separately. The investment in one results in the creation of the other. Such projects also require the introduction of landscape as a mediating condition.

Proliferation

Ambitions and boundaries. Architecture's desire to exceed itself—its formal, economic, and scalar constraints—is at once its most admirable characteristic and the source of so many of its greatest struggles. Since the idea of total design can apply as much to a domestic interior as to the globe, architecture's proliferative impulse requires precise channels.

Kenneth Frampton: A megaform is by definition restricted in its extent. It may thus be realized by the society, in a limited time period as a one-off urban intervention capable of affording a programmatically different experience within the seemingly infinite, space-endlessness of the contemporary megalopolis.[15] (2010)

Preston Scott Cohen: Rockefeller Center is one-off, singular, episodic. It has no ambition to proliferate and become systemic or boundless. As opposed to architecture, the urban begs to be bounded. Its ambition is to not have a limit, but it must come to terms with having a limit if it's not going to participate in an inherited system. Architecture and urbanism each move toward the other. If urbanism is going to exist as something other than a system that is truly efficient, then it has to be more like architecture. It must be bound and it has to come to terms with being bound even as it aspires toward limitlessness. Architecture is moving in the opposite direction. It moves from the tradition of being discrete toward the ambition to include within itself all that by which the city has traditionally been defined. The discreteness of Rockefeller Center suggests that it is architecture trying to be a city, whereas Raymond Hood's Manhattan 1950 is urbanism trying to be architecture. This plan is the manifestation for the desire for an urban idea to turn into architecture, yet what will allow it to exist as urbanism lies in the specific organizations of the buildings themselves and the ways in which they can be synthesized with infrastructure.

Via Appia, by Appius Claudius
Caecus, Rome, constructed
mid-fourth century BCE

Keller Easterling: Architects have long worked on the production of
"object forms," but object forms and "active forms" can work
together. We can conceive of active forms as being composed of
repetitive populations of things or ecologies of pieces. My interest
in active form is not a critique of object form, but a suggestion that
we begin to explore the other half of what we as architects get to do.

Hashim Sarkis: The category of the urban is not very productive
anymore. If by "urban" we mean intense, complex, and diverse,
why is it that we are still operating with the concept in such a
singular manner? With the advent of globalization, we are told that
worldwide systems of economic exchange, political association, and
demographic flows are overwhelming the practices we associate
with the nation-state. Why is it that when it comes to architecture,
we have to stick to the city as the expression of globalization? The
importance of the megaform/megastructure debate is that it begins
to unpack the city as an entity from its internal constituents, but
also from the scale of outreach and impact. I am not saying that the
urban will or should disappear. All I am saying is that we should be
able to look at New York, Tokyo, and London and see something
other than a centralized city, an intensely centralized and big city,
but centralized nevertheless. Rome was at once city and empire.
The Colosseum and the Via Appia managed to move between
several scalar conceptions between city and empire and between
architecture and infrastructure. I am interested in exploring these
possibilities and I'm not sure that the debates we have in front
of us today, whether about the disciplinary boundaries or about the
return to the urban, are going to expand on these possibilities.

Utopia

The alternative reality function. A siren of the distant future or past, utopia animates architectural speculation, while foreclosing other potentials in the present. Adopted at times as a heuristic device and at others as an ideological implement, utopia is an impulse to be reckoned with at a moment when the construction of cities from scratch is becoming more viable than addressing extant conditions head-on.

Colin Rowe: Given the recognition that utopian models will founder in the cultural relativism which, for better or worse, immerses us, it would seem only reasonable to approach such models with the greatest circumspection; given that the inherent dangers and debilitations of any institutionalized status quo—and particularly a status quo ante (more of a Levittown, more of a Wimbledon, even more of Urbino and Chipping Camden)—it would also seem that neither simple "give them what they want" nor unmodified townscape are equipped with sufficient conviction to provide more than partial answers; and, such being the case, it becomes necessary to conceive of a strategy which might, one hopes, and without disaster, accommodate the ideal which might plausibly, and without devaluation, respond to what we believe the real may be.[16] (1984)

Preston Scott Cohen: Architecture always proposes an alternative to the common grounds of its context. Perhaps this ambition is utopian. I might be a believer in the distinction between the capital "A" and the little "a" of architecture even if I don't think there's a clear way to draw the line. If you take something like the idea of the vernacular, we understand that there's a limit beyond which we know that we're no longer operating within a set of conventions. There's a way to move toward making an exception, but then something happens and you've gone too far and you're no longer operating within the vernacular. When architecture moves beyond that limit, that's when we get the capital "A" architecture. The capital

"A" needs the definition of the little "a." When urbanism does this, it's also beginning to act the way architecture does. At a certain point beyond the limits of convention a project such as Tange's proposal for Tokyo Bay becomes just "other," unmistakably "other." There's no way to confuse such a move with participating within the preexisting condition of the city. I hate to say it, but I think that the utopian project actually requires a naïve belief in the possibility of the realization of its vision. This type of project will always be more like architecture than urbanism. It's fated to materialize as a fragment since it will always be surrounded by something that it can't control.

Reyner Banham: [On Kenzo Tange's project for Tokyo Bay] The sense of scale is unnerving; so is the formal control over all the parts of the professedly aformal and uncontrollable megaform.[17] (1976)

Keller Easterling: I don't react well to the word "utopia" at all. I don't permit the word. I just don't believe in it. It's the one rather than the many. It excludes. There's just a temperament of righteousness around that word that I don't find productive. It's a red herring that confuses a conversation and is all too easily co-opted by authoritarian power. Utopianism is one engine of successive rather than coexistent intelligence—binaries of opposing notions where this kills that. One can track it to track a history of Modernism, but it is an unnecessary, even mistaken, habit of mind.

Le Corbusier: Things are not revolutionized by making revolutions. The real Revolution lies in the solution of existing problems.[18] (1929)

Nader Tehrani: The relationship between the mega-project and utopia depends on how the former is historicized. In the scale of the mega-project as conceptualized in the early to mid-twentieth century, pieces of infrastructure seemed to have a kind of visionary status in their time, but have become quite miniature compared to what's being produced today. The utopian has become brutally real and is now institutionalized within a developed bureaucracy that sustains that very scale today. And so the question is to what degree can a vision be sustained under those terms, because the power of singularity has, more often than not, come to be compromised in the process. Another utopian vision may lie in the possibilities of design by community or design by politics, or in finding ways of creating something that is not only architecturally, but also socially, larger than the sum of its parts. Architects must now figure out how to do a project that has that capacity to wield such specifications at various levels at this new scale that has been delivered to us.

Felipe Correa: The utopias of the recent past sought to propose a very different way of inhabiting the world apart from the city. The task now, as suggested by the High Line, is less about coming up with something from scratch, but rather is in understanding how you can insert or introduce alternative identities into the city, and doing so with an as-built condition that already brings a given hand of cards to the table.

High Line, by James Corner Field Operations, Diller Scofidio + Renfro, and Piet Oudolf, New York, 2009

Conduct

**Connection | Synthesis | Multiplication |
Valency | Evolution**

Connection

**Linkages and directions. Intrinsically bound with
issues of infrastructure, connection assumes
both literal and symbolic qualities. Though the
meandering line of Le Corbusier may rightfully
speak to the architectural imagination, sectional
and networked linkages may exert greater force
while eluding coherent visual representation.**

Keller Easterling: I'm always worried about using the term "infrastructure," but I still seem to find myself using it. We think we know what
infrastructure is, but it refers to so much. There are economists
and McKinsey consultants and analysts for the World Bank who are
effectively making space. As architects, we're the ones who know
something about space and we could be the ones writing those
protocols and figuring out those interdependencies. We can make
very intelligent stones in the water. It's a very reasonable architectural choice to just want to do that. But, some of us are also curious
about the water itself.

Paul Lewis: The master plan is interesting in that it deals with movement primarily through the horizontal. Could a master-section
be a potential tool? The section is where architects take on greater
specificity and efficacy, and also operate in more complex ways with
infrastructure. The megaform is inherently positioned to address
the section.

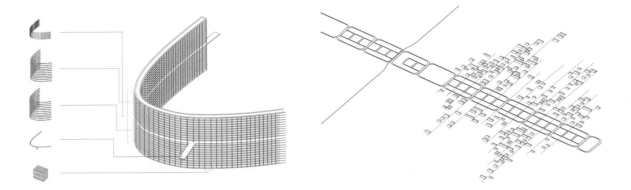

Felipe Correa: The term "megastructure" means something very different today than when Banham was theorizing it. The idea of being able to create a project that has spatial coherence without necessarily having literal formal continuity is an interesting conception of what a megastructure can be. Wacker Drive in downtown Chicago is a megastructure in the sense that there's a larger infrastructural base that allows it to accommodate multiple hands in terms of the individual buildings that occupy it. As a fragment of the city, Wacker Drive is a very successful urban project.

Analysis of Le Corbusier's Plan Obus for Algiers, by Alexandria Lee, 2011

Analysis of Kenzo Tange's Tokyo Bay Plan, by Matt Scarlett, 2011

Vincent Scully: The towers [of the Brooklyn Bridge] are still mid-century Gothic, sharp and linear, but the roadway sweeps out into the new continuity of space which was to be the salient feature of the architecture of Richardson, Sullivan, and Wright, and hence America's major contribution to the first phases of international modern architecture in the early twentieth century. The bridge itself towered over the city; the curve of its road cut high above the old buildings. So it introduced all at once the scale of a new urban world and released into space its symbol of the roadway rushing continuously onward.[19] (1969)

Drawing of Le Corbusier's Plan Obus for Algiers, by Alexandria Lee, 2011

Synthesis

Prospects of unity. New scales of political and economic action offer untold potentials for the integration of the built environment, yet frictions always emerge. Here, at the moment of the technical possibility of its realization, the question of synthesis returns to the origins of its assumptions.

Reyner Banham: In the guise of "urban design," the exercise of architecture on a very large scale might bridge the gap between the single building and its disintegrating urban context. It was this belief that brought together such unlikely partners as Italian hill-towns, Jersey tank farms, Victorian seaside piers and stranded aircraft-carriers in a single argument. Each in some way asserted that a physically comprehensible form, however rich and indeterminate, exists for urban building problems, as against the "incomprehensible sprawl" of the simplistic, unfocused, statistical city of single-family dwellings on a million suburban lots.[20] (1976)

Manhattan 1950, Montage of
Aerial Photograph and Drawing,
by Raymond Hood, 1929

Roadtown, Sketch,
by Edgar Chambless, 1910

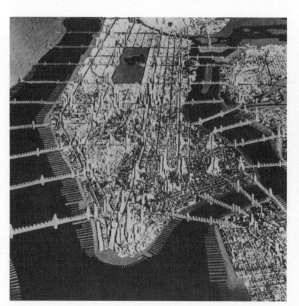

Edgar Chambless: The Roadtown is a scheme to organize production, transportation and consumption into one systematic plan. In an age of pipes and wires, and high speed railways such a plan necessitates the building in one dimension instead of three—the line distribution of population instead of the pyramid style of construction. The rail-pipe-and-wire civilization and the increase in the speed of transportation is certain to result in the line distribution of population because of the almost unbelievable economy in construction, in operation and in time.[21] (1910)

Nader Tehrani: China is evolving at a pace that makes the speed at which Route 95 connected Maine to Florida almost tepid in its rational, procedural, and incremental way over the years and decades that made that scale achievable. It somehow happened in correspondence with the speed of cars. I think the biggest challenge right now has to do with acknowledging that the necessity of the proximity of real estate to infrastructure produces conditions like those found in Hong Kong and Shenzhen, places that are expanding by the day and not by the decade. The question then becomes how do you mobilize the large-scale thinking going on within the architectural discipline to address the political urgencies of places that have rapidly developing economies? The degree to which you can orchestrate the forces of hybridity has to do either with the way in which you can be there as an architect to absorb all of the disciplines under your own umbrella or, conversely, the degree to which you can make the different disciplines coalesce around the singularity of a civic ambition, the figure that holds it all together. What's at stake here is the ability of architects to specify the definition of our media and our discipline through organizational, material, and spatial means in order to change the current reality of how cities work. The hybridity of infrastructure, if considered through the lens of architecture rather than planning or civil engineering, offers a seductive means by which we can begin to specify this transformation of the city.

Multiplication

Intensification and added value. Through appropriation or by design, architecture possesses latent abilities to elevate a situation from ordinary to extraordinary. Such animation may take on a monumental character, but can just as well emerge from a minute adjustment in the conventional urban landscape.

Keller Easterling: An aesthetics of the object is different from an aesthetics of practice. What Rancière would call an "aesthetic practice" is something that cannot be represented visually. In fact, you wouldn't actually want to represent such a practice in this way, because that's not the intent. It's not about the literal translation of, say, a rhizome into a weave of fingers; that's not the fun of it. Approaching a landscape, for example, you would not attempt to interact with the system by wiring all the branches of every tree, but rather you would send something in that you knew was part of the interdependent ecology, and your great pleasure would come from seeing how that element interacted and modified the system. It wouldn't be about resolution, nor would it be a project of drawing and representing all the different interactions, but rather the pleasure would be in producing a kind of growth in the landscape. You let one germ work its way throughout the site, and then you introduce something else.

Then again, we're also architects and we want to make form, so all of the pleasures of geometry and shape should make their way into this "other" aesthetic practice. We don't have to abandon the habits of the discipline or start again. We make the stuff, but we can make stuff perform as well.

Nader Tehrani: Isn't it somehow true of all architecture and urbanism that when the figurative power of certain spatial or formal conditions becomes visible, questions of how they're occupied,

Chicago Convention Hall
Project, by Mies van der Rohe,
1954

what programs they sponsor, and the ways in which they are
meant to be used matters less? It's in those moments when projects
sponsor the ability to become public and multivalent in ways that
were never anticipated by the scenographic manner in which we
draw them. Consider Jürgen Mayer's canopy in Seville after Spain
won a recent European football championship match. Were you
to Photoshop something like that it would come closest to the
famous Mies collage of his proposed convention hall, where a very
abstract, silent void becomes an attendant volume for appropriation. The championship celebration was really the moment for
Jürgen's project, as if to legitimate it purely on the grounds of that
event. This discourse on the formal power of infrastructure is
interesting in that it suggests the capacity of something to outlive its
function and to exist in a perpetual state of "becoming." The colosseum in Lucca, for example, is a powerful urban form, but Aldo
Rossi considered it to be a great piece of infrastructure as well. Rossi
understood that organizational form has an ability to sponsor centuries and centuries of alternative lives.

Keller Easterling: The challenge is in identifying the right kind of
"multiplier" for existing site conditions.

Preston Scott Cohen: Some of the reaction to my canopy project in Battery Park City has emphatically suggested that it is not a work of architecture. Granted, it doesn't have all the fundamentals; it doesn't have mechanical systems, it doesn't have rooms, it doesn't have a thermal interior. At the same time, I never once considered it to be something other than architecture even though on nearly every level it acts as an urban element—as an object that might partake in the definition of urban space. One could compare it somewhat to Grand Central Station in that it's a big room. Had the form offered a less generous spatial quality, it would not have the same effect. Architecture has the unique capacity to define moments of provisional or actual interiority. In the case of Grand Central, it feels like a piece of city interiorized. Conversely, the canopy is continuous with the whole of the city, but it evokes architecture. It's the evocation of architecture as interior without manifesting it.

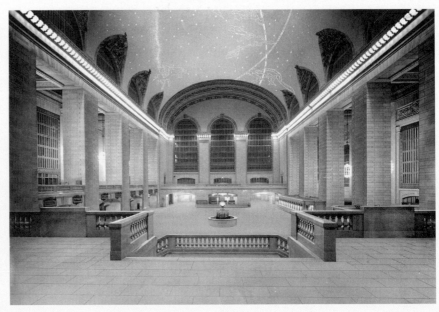

Arcade Canopy, by Preston
Scott Cohen, New York, 2012

Grand Central Station,
by Reed and Stem, Warren
and Wetmore, New York, 1913

Valency

Object reverberations and hybrid acts. Here, the efficacy of an architectural act is a function of the way in which it concentrates physical and perceptual linkages across multiple scales and constituencies.

Paul Lewis: If architects want to act in the city, then we have to identify or generate other architectural models—other sections—that continue to push the public beyond the street. There have to be alternative diagrams or organizational questions that engender the possibility for architecture to foster public engagement. This ambition to induce socialization within the building brings forward issues involving programming and intensification. Then the question becomes, at what point are such strategies being deployed in such a controlled and manufactured way that they ultimately offer a false freedom? The desire is to induce exchanges that go beyond the control of the architect. I'm always very interested in the specificity of something. To simply jam programs together doesn't always work. The question is: how are these elements being choreographed in a very particular way? Grand Central and the current Penn Station do arguably the same thing, but Penn's failures are entirely architectural, they're not infrastructural. They both have train tracks, they both have multiple levels, and they both have to get "x" many people in and out. They are alike in terms of their infrastructure, but architecturally, one is fantastic and one is a disaster.

Hashim Sarkis: Since at least the emergence of the picturesque, the difference between the performative and the aesthetic has long been a central debate in the theory of art. On this issue, I side with the Romantics and with Keats. The "negative capabilities" of our art are all we have to give us assurance that we are able to operate effectively in the increasingly uncertain contexts of our practice. In Keats, based on Vendler, we have three eyes observing the artwork: one wants to situate the artwork in its historical and geographic

Housing for the Fisherman of
Tyre, by Hashim Sarkis Studios,
Abbasiyeh, 2008

context, one wants it to produce perceptual effects, and a third looks
for the rules of the object's own making, to watch it intensify from
within, to allow for an internal but alternative reality to emerge. It is
this internal, perhaps more radical, realism that sways me more to
the megaform. There is something too organicist about megastructures and about performative thinking in architecture. I am not able
to accept that if something blends in or looks like it is blending in,
then it is going to make a difference.

Nader Tehrani: In my practice over the years I've struggled with
the notion of inevitability through construction and with finding
construction systems that have the ability to produce reciprocity
between part and whole. This happens sometimes in the early projects through responsive skins; later they go into 2 ½ dimensional
systems like the Kuwait project [Villa Moda] where structure,
span, and organization create connections between the cell of a
building type and the megaform of the whole, and then we get into
the more spatial strategies of our Issam Fares Institute where the
modularity of variable geometries begins to create spatial envelopes
that engage the structure, program, circulation, and building
systems all at once. Between manner and convention, the middle
ground I'm hoping for is reciprocity, where questions of symbolic
performance and the technical mandates of an architecture
that would otherwise be value-engineered out of the discipline
are brought into collusion such that they coalesce the necessary
forces into a compelling whole, and from there you might begin to
shave off some fat if necessary.

Felipe Correa: The city has always been driven by capital, but how that capital is given shape has to do with the different agents that participate and the values that are brought into the equation. In the context of the American city, we've seen a shift from infrastructure being the backbone of development (the grid, the construction of levees) toward purely private agents fulfilling that role. The task of the mega-project today is to begin to rethink the set of values that might lead to another shift in power. To a certain extent, issues of ecology and sustainability achieved their prominence within the architectural discipline because they do begin to impact the broader balance of power between public and private interests. What we need to understand is that spatial ideas can alter this balance as well. Architects are essential actors in the mega-project because we can bring qualities to the city that private development cannot or will not provide by itself.

Analysis of James Corner Field Operations, Diller Scofidio + Renfro, and Piet Oudolf's High Line, by Miriam Parera, 2011

Evolution

Resilience and the remodeling of growth. Ultimately, the success of the large-scale project will rely on its ability to nurture both its own evolution and that of its urban surroundings. Designs for such interventions require an intelligent negotiation of the anticipated temporal and socioeconomic frictions that will impact a project's maturation and afterlife.

Fumihiko Maki: If the megaform becomes rapidly obsolete, as well it might, especially in those schemes which do not allow for two kinds of change cycle, it will be a great weight about the neck of urban society.

The ideal is not a system, on the other hand, in which the physical structure of the city is at the mercy of unpredictable change. The ideal is a kind of master form which can move into ever new states of equilibrium and yet maintain visual consistency and a sense of continuing order in the long run. This suggests that the megastructure which is comprised of several independent systems that can expand or contract with the least disturbance to others would be more preferable to the one of a rigid hierarchical system.[22] (1964)

Felipe Correa: When we talk about the evolutionary structure of a project the idea is not simply to rethink the structure of the whole, but also to consider how phasing can be incorporated into the design strategy from the very beginning, rather than viewing it as something that gets staged as a sequence of events once the design process is complete.

The biggest difficulty in phasing a megastructure has to do with the separation between public and private. If you can actually calibrate those conditions adequately, there is a possibility of a particular phasing. The most interesting set of mega-projects are those in which phasing is intrinsic to the structure of the project. In the Malagueira Housing project, for example, Alvaro Siza created the infrastructural spine and basic services such that even though the market is what defines the growth of housing over time, the logic of that growth is intrinsic to the design of the project.

We should, however, distinguish between phasing and participation. The problem that often arises with public participation in cities is that sometimes you have the biggest debates over nothing, because there is nothing there to discuss. If the discussion starts with an idea, as radical as it might be, there is a point of reference against which things can be measured.

Nader Tehrani: Rafael Moneo's souk project in Beirut is an interesting case in the context of infrastructure and megaform. Traditionally, the souks were extremely vital as the urbanistic core of the city and they were organized along different streets or alleyways, each of which sold different products; the vegetables on one corridor, the copper smiths on another, the clothes, the meats, etc. And by the time you occupy all these axes you have a plaid array of market-places in a tight-knit proximity. Here, the fabric of the physical form of the souks and the continuity they produce with the city has a direct relationship with the economies that sustain them. There was a war that bombed out the souks, yet the basic footprints of them remained. At the same time, there were also city conditions around this infrastructural footprint that arguably needed to be maintained as a way of energizing and integrating the site with the new city. The difficulty with all this is that the new souks do not and cannot have the same marketplace that once existed there. The bombing didn't simply level the built environment of the city; it also destroyed the very social fabric that sustained the city and its marketplace. So now, almost by necessity, Beirut has a mall that's in the middle of the city and ironically, Moneo's task was not to recreate the souks, but rather to de-materialize the mall. As a mall, it's relatively small, but the way in which it has been cut through, ruptured, integrated, and made to centrifugally re-engage the city in section and in plan make it singular at one moment, but also multiple at another. Moneo understood that were he to attempt to recreate the souk, he was bound for failure, so the only thing he could do was to re-invent the mall, which is inevitably what the project became. Though it doesn't succeed on many levels, it is smart in how it relates to very real issues of the continuous versus the fragmented; the singular versus the compartmentalized; the civic versus the privatized; all of those things that produce the tensions and impossibilities of the utopian.

Preston Scott Cohen: Originally, I think, the move to preserve the High Line had to do with the historicism, the lament, the loss of the potential and the friction that was caused by the uninhabitable, unforgiving presence of industrial infrastructures that can't be integrated with our lives in a clean way. The waterfront was a territory that was off-limits for a long time, but it promised a kind of unknown. It was a very eroticized, dark, decadent side of urbanity that was lost. The sentiment to rescue it through preserving fragments of industrial obsolescence was intended to keep alive something that once seemed full of mystery. Of course, the High Line became something else. It's beautiful now and you don't feel the industrial past. Some would find it difficult to fetishize something that did harm to the urban fabric, and in fact, the High Line still does cause harm, in a way. The underside does not produce good spaces. And, on another level, nobody can stand to live next to that much public scrutiny. There needs to be the capacity on the upper level to let you off into the flanking buildings. How can you program it otherwise? As it is now, it's not actually a model of urbanism. It's a one-off and the one-off is a great attractor because it foils the general condition of the city that we take for granted.

Nader Tehrani: There are few infrastructural opportunities where we are able to productively engage many pieces of architecture through a kind of form. The success of the High Line does not come from the design alone. The design is elegant and we like it, but its power and its utopian possibilities come from the fact that its structure preexisted and someone didn't have to propose it. It only needed

Alison and Peter Smithson: The greatest difficulty in working towards urban forms that can accept growth and change is that of communicating the general intention to those who will follow. The apparent unwillingness or inability of many people to accept general rules might make an open-ended approach impossible except as an aesthetic in the hands of a single practitioner. Yet for a considerable period, the orders of architecture were so universally accepted that they made the whole of the built environment cohesive, no matter how many hands contributed. Throughout our work we have thought about a plan that could present a non-rigid idea, a way of indicating by means of drawings, a direction that an urban form could take. These drawings could suggest possibilities that might accrue or become obvious only when the first portion had been built.[23] (1992/2002) more programming from below and above and on the linear axis of the city. If the High Line hadn't existed, I doubt that anyone would have conceptualized it as a necessity. Is it inventive at the formal level and programmatic level? Probably not enough, but then it's okay, because you're dealing with an industrial relic in a dense city where its elevation is seen as a relief from the street.

Paul Lewis: If the nature of a megastructure is that it evolves, then the architect's role is to negotiate that evolution. The way you do that intelligently is through a very close inspection of what's there; aiming not to preserve it, repeat it, or reconstitute it, but rather to alter it in a very dramatic and powerful way. From an architectural standpoint, working on an existing set of structures is fundamentally different than designing from the ground up, because what you do is to set in motion a fantastic oscillation between two conditions that allow you to design something you can't do in isolation. Even at a smaller scale, it's exciting to modify existing buildings because unexpected frictions emerge that permit you to design something like a single-story office space with forty foot high ceilings because you're modifying an old maintenance building. You would never do that if you were building an economically efficient office building from the ground up. I would argue that much of the possibility of the new urban environment will be produced through the negotiation of such frictions. Embracing friction also suggests a different lens through which to consider the idea of evolution. Rather than the survival of the fittest, we should foreground evolution as a set of failures, where it's the flaws and frictions that end up actually moving things along. How, then, do we induce these sorts of mistakes intelligently?

Preston Scott Cohen: The wonderful thing about large-scale infrastructural conditions is that they're not designed by a single person at a single moment. They don't operate as a kind of utopia, but rather are an accumulation of things. The idea of evolution here is one that continuously pushes up against the ideal and moves it into a different direction.

Social Infrastructures

Marion Weiss | Michael A. Manfredi

Virtual or physical, systems that aggregate individuals and ideas are institutional forums with indefinite boundaries. As virtual systems exponentially multiply, the value of the physical space of academic, professional, and cultural institutions is being debated globally. But just as the paperless paradigm anticipated by the advent of the digital was never realized, the virtual workplace/academic institution/urban center has not eliminated, but rather amplified the efficacy of shared space to advance ideas. Images of New York City's Occupy Wall Street at Zuccotti Park and Hong Kong's Umbrella Sit-in illuminate the ideological common ground catalyzed by social media, manifest in distinctly public settings, and dispersed again through images legible to a global audience.

Against this evolving backdrop, academic, professional, and cultural institutions are questioning the quantitative and qualitative values of shared, loose-fit space as economic pressures, limited physical space, and demands for efficiency converge as they build for unforeseen futures dedicated to research and capitalized creativity. These pressures have led many institutions to value increasingly distilled program-specific buildings, but this apparent efficiency carries the risk of instituting physical and philosophical "blind spots." Just as the modern office is adjusting to the "work everywhere" approach and academic models are fusing with entrepreneurial agendas, we believe there is increasing value in creating purposeful inefficiencies in the connecting spaces, amplifying visual and physical connections, particularly where the geographic segregation of multistory spaces can preclude engagement.

Institutional campuses are currently undergoing a significant transformation. Universities, corporations, museums, and medical complexes are expanding their programs and ambitions against the context of limited physical resources. Once stable and clearly defined, these institutions are now operating at an increasingly large scale and often in preexisting urban settings where growth is provisional, haphazard, and opportunistic. In 1970 the Smithsonian Museums hosted 13.4 million visitors. By 2013 that number grew to over 30 million. Similarly, the number of students attending urban universities has increased by over 40 percent between 2010 and 2014. The converging and often contradictory forces of growth, limited resources, and evolving identities demand an intelligent approach to the complex spatial and functional needs of the contemporary campus.

"Campus" derives from the Latin word for "field," and although this definition has its associations with the pastoral (traditional exurban campuses like Princeton and the University of Virginia come to mind), it has little currency in describing campuses that are increasingly urban. Beyond simply a matter of internal organization, the efficacy of the contemporary campus is determined in large part by siting. Located in or near major urban centers so as to take advantage of the amenities and transportation services crucial to attracting talent, institutions have a certain responsibility to the cities on which they depend. The planning

University of Virginia, designed by Thomas Jefferson, engraving by H. Weber, Charlottesville, Virginia, 1856 and design of "campus" projects is an opportunity to forge a bond across a broader and more diverse range of constituents, institutional actors, programs, and scales of interaction. The emerging hybrid of the research university, for example, creates a new set of architectural issues and opportunities. Here, producing clearly delineated building typologies within finite site boundaries is no longer relevant or possible.

Although the research campus is perhaps the most visible manifestation of a broader transformation in patterns of work and education, traditional institutions of higher learning, medical complexes, and museums are also assuming increasingly important roles as economic engines, and the facilitation of their continued evolution poses its own set of design challenges. And, though developments in digital technology have forced institutions of every kind to reevaluate their priorities in programming, amenity provision, research protocols, and space needs, specific responses depend on the nature of the institution. The communal and pedagogical spaces that foster the open-ended study of a liberal arts college are not always conducive to the needs of a major research university where collaboration becomes essential. At the same time, however, such divergence of needs allows us to consider the ways in which each form of learning and organization can cross-pollinate the other.

Despite their evident differences, nearly all institutions share constraints on property and available resources. New construction can rarely be accommodated in the heart of historical campus settings without displacing existing buildings or recreation spaces, necessitating either careful incision or the siting of new work on the edges of campus. If the Diana Center at Barnard College is an example of the former, our Krishna P. Singh Center for Nanotechnology at the University of Pennsylvania engages the latter condition. Although not outwardly infrastructural in size, these projects participate in the reorientation of their respective campuses—the first by concentrating activity within a new center and the second by establishing a peripheral locus of activity and reinforcing the spine of campus that connects the university to the larger city.

Scale, Form, and Performance: Contradictions and Compatibilities

Many of our projects for educational and research institutions, such as the Diana Center, the Singh Center, and the North American headquarters for Novartis, are individual buildings that, by virtue of their siting and design, participate in and shape their larger respective precincts. The language of architecture is often too singular to address new and changing programs, whereas the language of planning is not specific enough to address the nuances of site and scale. Both fall short and necessitate the development of new design strategies, new languages. In this emergent context we advocate acupunctural design strategies that register a big impact. These strategies are infrastructural in ambition and performance rather than scale. They also recognize that the demand for a more ecological form of infrastructure goes hand-in-hand with the evolution of spaces devoted to other ecologies, other natures—those of research, learning, and community. Put another way, ecological concerns need not preclude the specific, fine-grained needs of art making, study, play, or even applied research. In fact, these activities generate their own parallel social ecologies—what Ian McHarg called the "biophysical social system."

Our interest in scale, form, and performance owes a debt to Fumihiko Maki, who, in his 1964 essay "Investigations in Collective Form," analyzed the values of compositional form, megastructure, and group-form as they related to clusters of buildings or city fragments. In writing of group-form, Maki argued: "Forms in group-form have their own built in link, whether

Hillside Terrace Complex,
by Fumihiko Maki, Tokyo, 1992

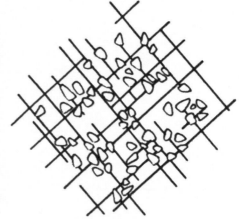

expressed or latent, so that they may grow in a system. They define basic environmental space which also partakes of the quality of systematic *linkage*. Group-Form and its space are indeed proto-type elements, and they are prototypes because of implied *system* and *linkage*" (our italics). We had the pleasure of discussing these concepts with Maki on several occasions, as well as witnessing how the ideas took shape in his brilliant Hillside Terrace project in Tokyo, where he maintains his office. After one of our visits, Maki suggested we step outside and leisurely walk the project over the course of that afternoon. Lacking an overt composition or organiza-tion, the project's gestalt is instead slowly revealed and refracted though a series of subtle, evocative adjustments: the reciprocity of inside-outside, opaque-transparent; a conversation framed by a steel scrim; a tree positioned so its changing shadows play across Maki's architecture. Movement creates linkages that are oblique, never frontal. One gradually slides into courtyards and buildings as the project expands and contracts. The shift from street to court-yard, canopy to corridor, wall to window, is bound together by a lightness of touch where edges dissolve and the architecture disap-pears and reappears. The project is large but its scale and affects telescope effortlessly. On our visit, we were struck by the scalar evolution of Hillside Terrace (built over thirty years) and its capacity to insert itself into its context without losing its figure or identity. Indeed, over time the project succeeds in creating its own context that is as much social as it is physical. The value for us is in the creation of forms that become catalytic agents to create connections or links to a much larger environment.

Similarly, in the context of our interest in scale and form we are drawn to Kenneth Frampton's argument for megaform as a stratagem for creating a vital and culturally significant place-form. He writes: "What is more pertinent in the case of the megaform is the topographic, horizontal thrust of its overall profile, together with the programmatic, place-creating character of its intrinsic program…the contemporary pertinence of this type is its landmark and place-making potential." Frampton's emphasis on a "quasi-catalytic function…the kind of urban intervention that stimulates hitherto unforeseen consequences" has been critical in developing our own work.[1]

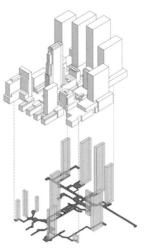

Rockefeller Center, by Raymond
Hood, Wallace K. Harrison, and
Max Abramovitz, New York, 1939

Right: Analysis of Rockefeller
Center, by Sarah Blitzer, 2014

Rockefeller Center is perhaps one of the most successful
examples of a megaform that inserts itself effortlessly into a preexisting context, in this case, the grid of midtown Manhattan. Here,
the figural core (central promenade and sunken court) stands
out against the grid and marks the center, whereas the project's
ambiguous edge weaves itself into the matrix of New York's block
structure. Living in New York, we often wander into the complex
from Sixth Avenue via 49th or 55th Street, where we're always
surprised to discover the project as if for the first time. Approaching
it from the subterranean level of the subway amplifies the topographic triumph of Rockefeller Center with a section that engages
each layer and strata of the city. For us, the power of Rockefeller
Center lies in its ability to simultaneously respond, disrupt, and
transform its context. It also reminds us of how architecture can
serve to model and facilitate broader urban transformations within
the infinite variety that lingers within the city's rigid grid.

Research and Innovation: Density and Friction

Geographers and economists have often noted the compatible
clustering of economic activity and innovation. Seeking to leverage
the benefits of density, universities, corporations, and research
institutions are increasingly gravitating toward dense urban centers.
Over the past four decades Cambridge's Kendall Square has been
transformed from an industrial neighborhood anchored by MIT
into a gargantuan high-tech and biomedical hub. Microsoft, Google,

Amazon, and Twitter all have research facilities around Kendall
Square, along with a host of small and midsize tech companies. More
recently, Kendall Square has blossomed into a biomedical research
district; more than two-million-square-feet of R&D labs
and biomedical office space was added to the area between 2007
and 2014.

    The best research is consistently produced when scientists are
working within close proximity of each other. Science has ceased
to be a solitary endeavor, and researchers collaborate because they
know that the most interesting mysteries lie at the intersection
of disciplines. Research has established that—at multiple scales
ranging from city to workplace—density, mixed-use programming, and the clustering of people increases innovation, and with
it, patent production. "If you want people to work together effectively," argues Isaac Kohane of Harvard Medical School, an author
of a seminal study published by the Public Library of Science titled,
"Does Collocation Inform the Impact of Collaboration?" on the
effect of physical proximity, "[we] need to create architectures
that support frequent, physical, spontaneous interactions. Even
in the era of big science when researchers spend so much time on
the Internet, it is still so important to create intimate spaces."[2] If
the programmatic boundaries between pure research and applied
research, the academy and industry, campus and city are dissolving,
our spatial responses must adapt.

    The challenge here becomes one of effectively tuning the
anthropomorphics of space to create an architecture that amplifies
the frequency of programmed and spontaneous interactions. We
believe the architecture or infrastructure that supports research
should also enhance peripheral vision and catalyze positive spillover
effects crucial to innovation and creativity. In our project for the
Cornell/Technion campus on Roosevelt Island, the hourglass shape
of the building is configured to enhance the petri-dish marriage of
applied research and entrepreneurial endeavors, creating compression where circulation and sectional connections can generate
the potential for interpersonal frictions across diverse groups and
disciplines. By introducing programmatic juxtapositions—terraced
collaboration lounges incorporated into connecting stairs, river-
to-river spatial transparencies across lab and studio levels, and

interwoven circulation routes orchestrating increased frequency of those productive frictions—chance encounters capitalize creativity.

Identity: The Icon or the Quilt

Given the proliferation of images in our digital and physical environments, it comes as no surprise that institutions tend to foreground matters of iconography and branding. Unfortunately, in this context, the production of an architectural identity can quickly devolve into superficial image-making at the expense of more nuanced and layered gestures. Architecture can certainly work to create a brand or mirror an institution's preconceived history, but it can also challenge that history. It can introduce multiple meanings and multiple histories that do have collective value without succumbing to the allure of the logo.

For us, a meaningful approach to this conundrum lies in the mediation of type and site, function and affect. At the Krishna P. Singh Center for Nanotechnology, the architectural complex is organized around an ascending spiral that hybridizes the tradition of the campus quadrangle with the public promenade. Both the university and city of Philadelphia have a tradition of organizing buildings around open quads, yet laboratory buildings are typically organized around a linear corridor that affords little public space and even fewer spaces for interaction among researchers. The Center for Nanotechnology twists the laboratories around a central quad, opening the sciences to the university landscape and providing a suite of spaces for interaction. Here, multiple types—courtyard, laboratory loft, ascending gallery—each with their own distinct histories, are grafted together to create a new, but recognizable, hybrid. The center's identity emerges from this confluence of relationships rather than an overriding gesture.

Stability/Instability

Institutions are facing constant change. Flux and unpredictability are the norm, regardless of scale. At the scale of the campus, delineated boundaries and edges are porous, eroding distinctions between on- and off-campus spaces. At the architectural scale, the typical response to change is the now familiar trope of the neutral box that presumes a high level of flexibility. Non-generic spaces, however,

National Mall, by Pierre Charles
L'Enfant, Washington, D.C., 1791

often provide a level of character that offers traction and invites
change and inhabitation. In our Novartis project, the predominant
requirements for a flexible and changeable work space informed
the metrics of twenty-four-foot structural bays, eight-foot furniture
modules, and a comprehensive raised floor system. We chose to
strategically contrast these open, flexible work spaces with a series
of carefully delineated public rooms continuously interconnected by
amphitheater-like stairs and highly-modeled wood surfaces. Places
to eat, drink, gather, and pause create five distinct social destinations
within archipelagos of open office workstations.

In Manhattan, our design for Barnard College's Diana Center,
a seven-story creative arts building, transcends the intrinsic cultural
separations associated with multilevel buildings through a diagonally
interconnected series of double-height volumes. Avoiding the level-
by-level geographic separation that multifloor urban buildings can
create, these spaces carve through the building, creating strong visual
connections between distinctly different program elements and
departments, and enhancing a subliminal awareness of Barnard's
vibrant creative arts programs. A glass stair breaks free of the building's perimeter, connecting the diverse program centers at each level
and offering new views of the campus. This deliberate composition
of movement through a site and building can amplify the effects of
a space, create more open-ended relationships between architecture
and landscape, intensify the panoramic wonder of a vista, or offer a
highly edited refuge from the excess stimulus of everyday life. Rather
than a casual unfolding of one event after another, we are interested
in an experience of one event *because* of another. The levels and
movement patterns here not only connect and reveal site conditions,

they restructure their locations to allow them to be seen in new ways and transform the broader territories they engage.

As modes of work, study, recreation, and cultural production are increasingly intertwined, the role of such social infrastructures is shifting into an unknown territory. Forming the infrastructure of our beliefs, interests, and ambitions is a conviction that educational and cultural institutions are no less an inheritance than our physical environment. Architecture cannot outpace rapid developments in digital technology and the expanding social domain, but it can and should serve as a strategic partner in these efforts—an effective incubator for innovation capable both of anticipating its evolution and shaping its course toward more public ends. Resilient forms invite change and appropriation, privileging active engagement over passive reflection.

As we discovered with our project at the National Mall, not even monuments can exist in a vacuum. The site of the Sylvan Theater at the base of the Washington Monument serves at once as a frame for that towering obelisk, a concert venue, an offloading zone for tour buses, and a hinge point in a broader circuit linking the Mall to the memorials encircling the Tidal Basin to the south. As it currently stands, the site underperforms in each of these roles. Our design constructs a new topography that simultaneously conceals the sights and sounds of tour buses while bringing into focus the improbable backdrop of the stage and obelisk. A campus in the most fundamental sense of the word, the Mall is both historic artifact and a "campus" in a continually evolutionary state.

The transformation of such an exceptional public forum into a model for a more social form of civic engagement is perhaps the most overt demonstration of the kinds of changes we hope to effect with each of our projects, public or private. The portability of the social bridges high culture with the cultures of the workplace and the research institution, ensuring that well-designed projects induce effects that exceed their origins and proliferate throughout the urban environment. By approaching social infrastructures through a strategic lens, our practice encourages the development of new forms of connections, constructing objects and grounds that fundamentally alter those conditions when needs evolve. This infrastructural thinking reminds us of what a consensual thing a city and a campus can be.

Social Infrastructures

Barnard College Diana Center
Sylvan Theater at the Washington Monument
Novartis Headquarters Buildings
Cornell NYC Tech Co-Location Building
Krishna P. Singh Center for Nanotechnology

Barnard College Diana Center

New York, New York

From their desks in the glazed studio space
cantilevering from the Diana Center, students at
Barnard College have an expansive view down
Broadway, walled on its eastern edge by the
brick and limestone envelope of Charles McKim's
campus for Columbia University. Founded in 1889,
Barnard maintains an intimate four-acre campus
compressed within the dense urban environment
of Manhattan. The campus, composed of an
eclectic group of predominantly brick buildings,
is focused around Lehman Lawn with disconnected
landscape spaces at the periphery.

The Diana Center was designed to replace
Barnard's McIntosh Center, a brutalist concrete
structure designed in the 1960s that intentionally
disconnected the campus from the city as a means
of protecting its student population. Internally,
the McIntosh Center vertically severed the campus
into two distinct halves.

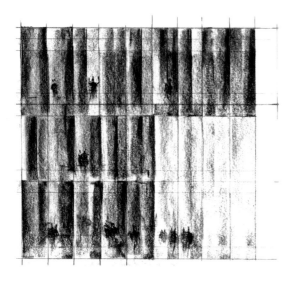

The Diana Center was tasked with reversing both of these measures, unifying a physically disconnected landscape while conversing with a historical one.

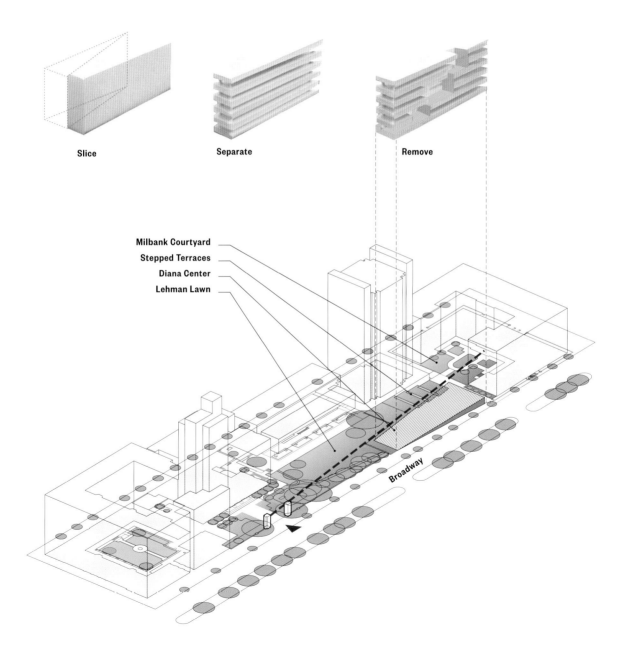

Slice

Separate

Remove

Milbank Courtyard
Stepped Terraces
Diana Center
Lehman Lawn

Broadway

From the historic entrance gate at Broadway, the building frames a clear sightline linking the central campus at Lehman Lawn to the lower-level historic core of the campus. Rethinking the mixed-use building type, the ninety-eight-thousand-square-foot multiuse building brings together the college's previously dispersed programs and constituencies by setting up visual juxtapositions that invite collaboration between disciplines.

The Diana Center establishes an innovative nexus for artistic, social, and intellectual life at the college, bringing together spaces for art, architecture, theater, and art history. The Diana Center's design extends Lehman Lawn horizontally and vertically, where a sculpted landscape of stepped terraces reestablishes a vital spatial continuity between the campus greens, which were previously separated by a fourteen-foot-high retaining wall and plaza. A place for performance, recreation, and study, the terraced lawn now enlivens the campus, turning a lack of available space into an opportunity to explore the site's sectional potential.

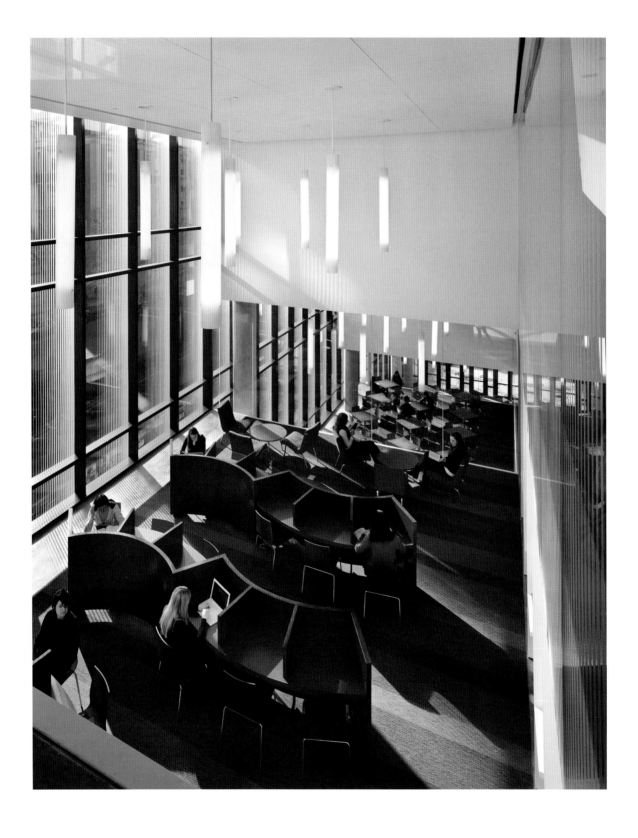

Carrying the sectional performance of the landscape into the building's interior, a diagonal void is carved through the building to form a cascading sightline that vertically unifies a gallery, reading room, dining room, and café at the ground level. This programmed view corridor of double-height glass atria ascends through the volume of the building, further transforming the generous spatial qualities of a conventional atrium. These spaces are furnished with a colorful interplay of custom-designed carrels, desks, and moveable lounge seating that invite adaptable modes of student use, offering a wide array of possibilities for individual and collaborative study. These adjoining spaces fuel spontaneous exchange among students and faculty from the diverse range of disciplines housed within.

Open views are maximized throughout the building, unveiling a continuous sightline through a layering of student spaces.

The building is the defining centralized place on campus for students, flexibly accommodating a range of uses from hosting spontaneous performances to conducting art installations. The building's enclosure establishes a reciprocal relationship between the campus context and the diverse program elements within the building. Assembled from 1,154 glass and copper-anodized aluminum panels, the envelope of the Diana Center is a shimmering terra-cotta colored field, broken at crucial moments by continuous transparent expanses. Parallel to the glass atria, an unfolded glazed staircase on the campus side of the building provides a dynamic setting for informal meetings and views to the surrounding campus landscape.

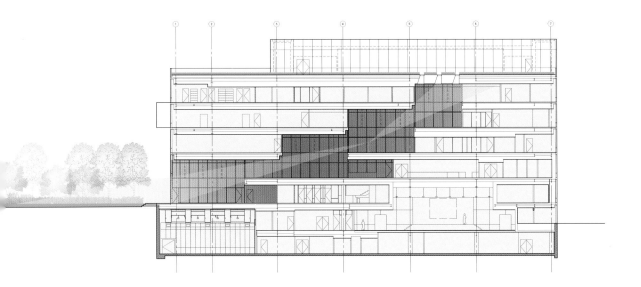

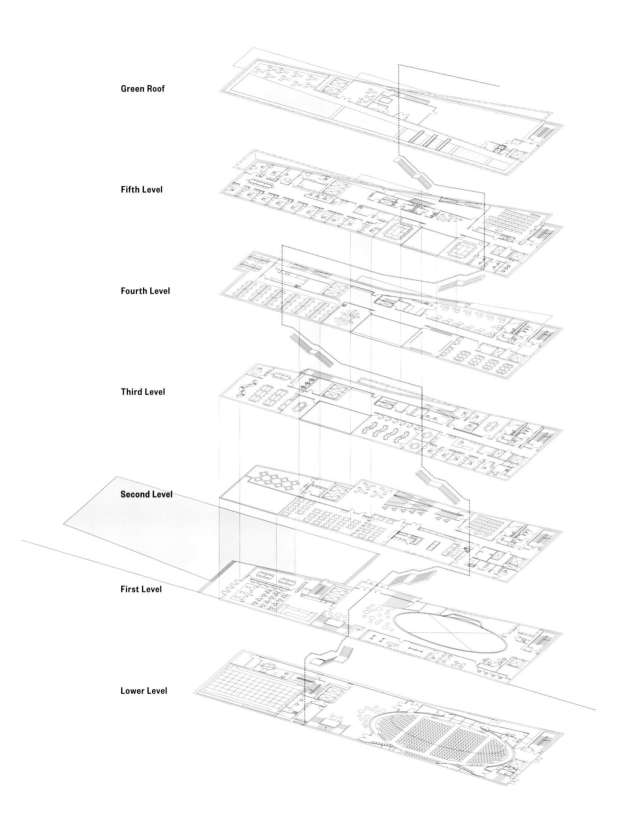

Green Roof

Fifth Level

Fourth Level

Third Level

Second Level

First Level

Lower Level

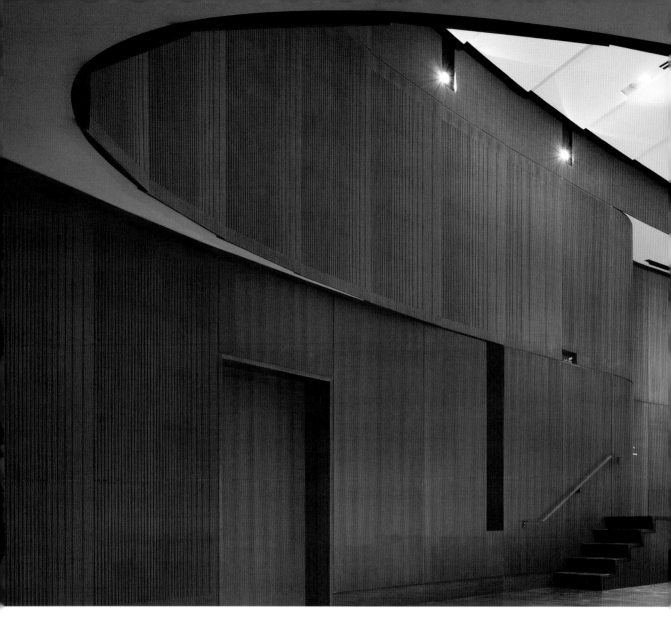

A five-hundred-seat multipurpose event space and one-hundred-seat black box theater anchor the lower levels and provide a flexible environment for lectures, special events, and theatrical productions.

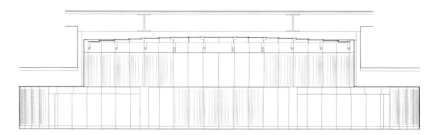

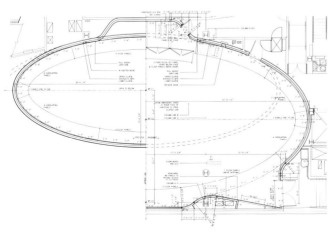

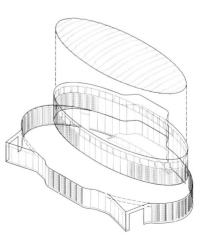

Conceived as a vertical campus quad, this cantilevered route weaves the spaces of the building into those of the campus. The chromatic richness of the acid-etched glass offers a means of mediating between the innovative aims of the center and the perennial poise of its historic institutional setting. Through the variation of color, opacity, and transparency calibrated to the center's internal programmatic needs, the facade invites views into the building's most public functions while limiting visibility to its more private spaces. Over the course of the day, changing environmental conditions and natural light exposure alter the tonal character of the building's surface. As manifest in the envelope, these layered effects combine to animate Barnard's street edge, conveying a sense of activity and openness that challenges the model of the cloistered urban campus, creating a luminous lens between the campus and the city.

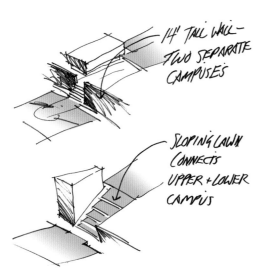

14' TALL WALL —
TWO SEPARATE
CAMPUSES

SLOPING LAWN
CONNECTS
UPPER + LOWER
CAMPUS

Marked by a fourteen-foot (4m) grade change and retaining wall, the division between Lehman Lawn to the south and the historic Milbank Hall to the north has long stood as an obstacle to social exchange in an otherwise close-knit academic community.

The chroma of the exterior glazing is calibrated to complement the material qualities of the historic buildings at Barnard and Columbia with a contemporary and energy-efficient curtain wall. Gradients of color, opacity, and transparency are created with fritted glass and color-integral panels that shift in hue and reflectivity throughout the changing light conditions of the day.

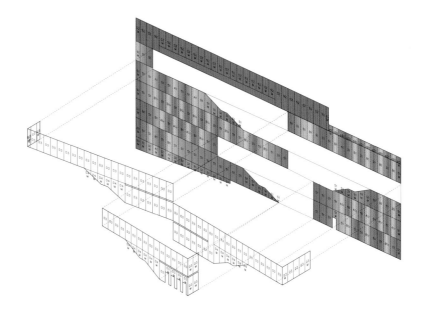

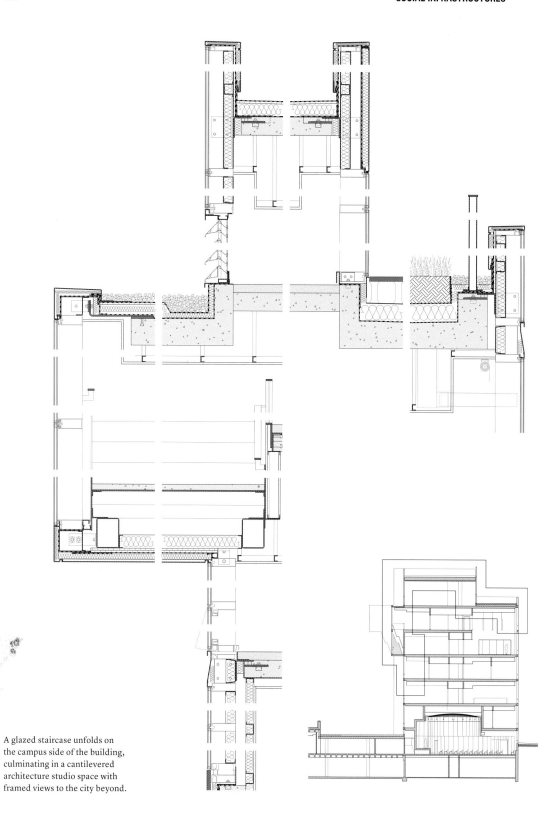

A glazed staircase unfolds on
the campus side of the building,
culminating in a cantilevered
architecture studio space with
framed views to the city beyond.

Sylvan Theater at the Washington Monument

Washington, D.C.

The National Mall in Washington, D.C., is the country's most symbolic public space, populated by monuments of national memory and L'Enfant's grand avenues. It is the site of the country's most powerful acts of civic pride and dissent—the center stage for events of historic resonance. Hosting over twenty-nine million visitors from around the globe each year, the Mall is an expansive landscape, a lumbering giant both enlivened and fatigued through use. On any given day, busloads of tourists are deposited along the sidewalks that line the grounds while crowds of museumgoers, politicos, protestors, and festival attendees simultaneously enliven the landscape. The green lawn bends to this exercise, its grass worn to dirt by photographers in the central spots where the dome of the Capitol appears on axis. Along the adjacent streets, fortified landscape elements sit alongside sculpture gardens, food vendors, and historical displays.

Sylvan Theater Site, 2012

A Historic Site: March on Washington, 1963

1   Washington Monument
2   Tidal Basin
3   Sylvan Amphitheater
4   Sylvan Pavilion
5   Pedestrian Woodland Walk

Amid this layered social setting at the heart of the Mall and visible for miles, the Washington Monument appears to rise above it all as the literal and philosophical compass for the nation. To the south of this defining landmark, the outdoor Sylvan Theater has become an increasingly orphaned setting with its back to the monument, compromised in recent years by a proliferation of roadways, tour buses, and security barriers. An open, public venue for the performing arts, the Sylvan Theater is a vital space for free artistic expression and entertainment in a town known more for its political debates.

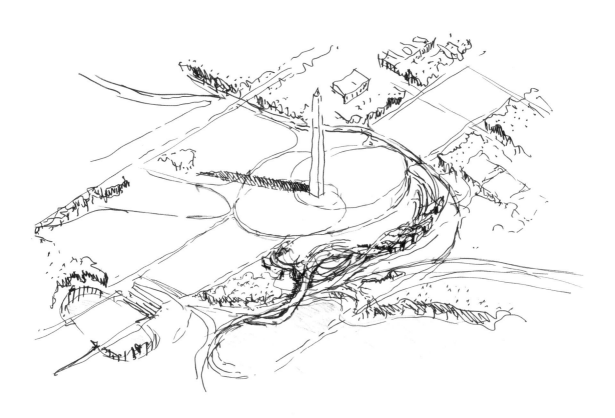

Standing in its present form as a wooden bandshell casually attached to a path that rings the base of the monument, the theater is consumed by the landscape developing around it and offers little in the way of views commensurable with the centrality of its site and the richness of its mission. The winner of a national competition, a new landform by Weiss/Manfredi and Olin transforms the site and reimagines how it might better function as both a performance venue and as a vehicle for improving the Mall's connection to the city's broader circuit of monuments and landscapes. Here, the Sylvan Theater becomes a grove, an active environment that restores the surprise and magic of the Shakespearean forest that inspired the name of the original theater nearly a century ago.

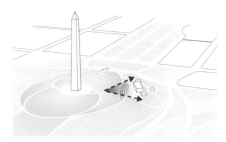

The existing Sylvan Theater

Reverse the orientation to frame views

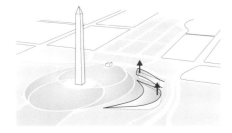

Sculpt the landscape to create an amphitheater

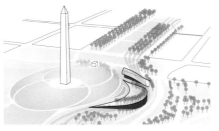

Provide amenities for shade, dining, and visitor services

The Sylvan Theater is oriented around a sequence of settings that together define a new performance landscape. The design reorients the theater to allow audiences a panoramic view of the Washington Monument, simultaneously elevating the audience and strategically concealing traffic and a queue of tour buses with an emerging topography. A new elevated pedestrian connection follows the upper contour of the amphitheater and connects to the nearby Tidal Basin and its celebrated cherry blossom promenade. This uppermost viewing terrace emerges as an aerial walk from the amphitheater, vaulting over an existing network of roadways and descending to the water's edge, to lead to the Thomas Jefferson, Franklin Roosevelt, and Martin Luther King Jr. memorials, creating a much larger visitor experience.

Monument Hillside:
Seating capacity 10,000+

Washington Monument

Security wall surrounds and
protects the monument hillside

Walkways separate performers
from the audience on the hillside

Tour buses queue behind
the theater, impairing
the view to the Jefferson
Memorial

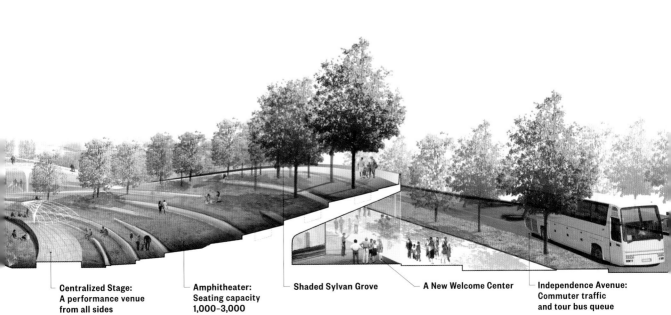

Centralized Stage:
A performance venue
from all sides

Amphitheater:
Seating capacity
1,000–3,000

Shaded Sylvan Grove

A New Welcome Center

Independence Avenue:
Commuter traffic
and tour bus queue

A terraced lawn and tree canopy structure the amphitheater, where a wide range of performances and events are seen against the towering backdrop of the Washington Monument. The tailored topography of the amphitheater supports performances of all scales. A slender amphitheater adjacent to the café offers a space for more intimate and spontaneous events, whereas the new Sylvan Theater hosts larger performances and, combined with the existing slope of the monument hillside, provides an open arena for audiences of thousands. The Sylvan Pavilion emerges from this landscape, providing an all-weather café and performance venue for visitors and a setting for gatherings and events. The pavilion bends along a pathway south to Independence Avenue, where a new exhibition gallery frames an arrival plaza for tour buses and an educational platform for the National Park Service.

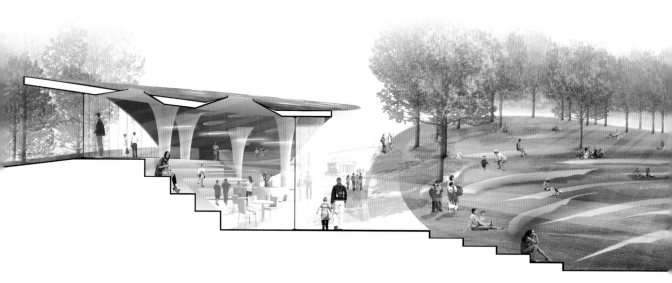

Inspired by the filtered light of a shaded forest, the pavilion's roof forms a canopy of dappled light. The terraced interior connects indoor and outdoor seating and performance venues.

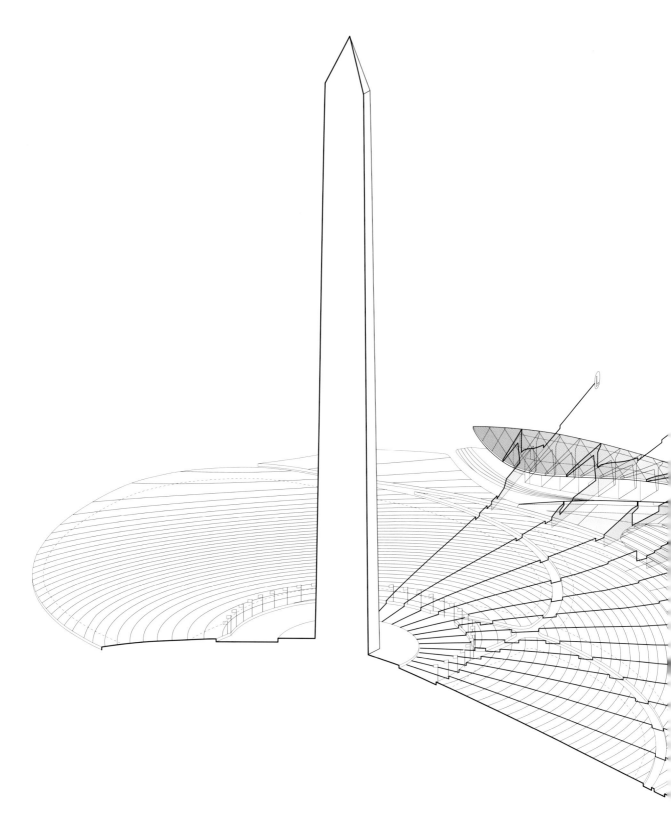

Supporting the proposed connection between the Mall and the Tidal Basin, the Sylvan Theater anticipates a future phase of the design that will expand its ecological performance through design measures aimed at improving traffic flows. Currently a network of roadways, this site for a new working landscape will provide a destination for the community and enable the development of a nursery that supplies plantings for the Mall. Here, landscape works alongside the city's museums and monuments to bring history alive and sustain the physical and social life of the national stage it animates.

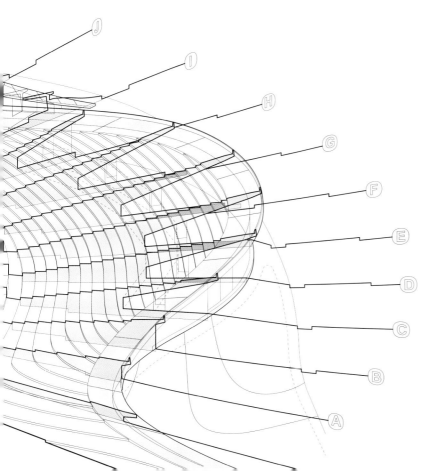

The Sylvan Theater's neighboring
landscapes are planted to establish
healthy urban ecological systems,
resiliently designed to thrive
under the Mall's high visitation
rates. Here, a high performance
landscape emerges, layered within
the diverse landscape settings
of the site.

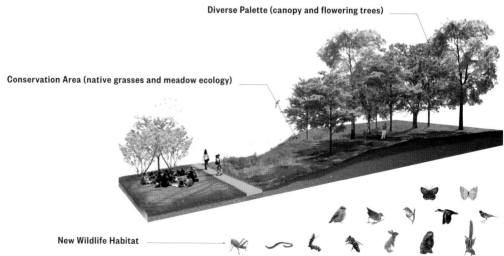

Diverse Palette (canopy and flowering trees)

Conservation Area (native grasses and meadow ecology)

New Wildlife Habitat

Novartis Headquarters Buildings

East Hanover, New Jersey

rs

Expressing a culture of innovation, the Novartis Corporation commissioned a group of internationally recognized architects to reimagine its 230-acre North American headquarters, as precedented by the corporation's recent transformation of its Basel campus. Departing from the model of the generic postwar American corporate campus, the reenvisioned headquarters offers an integrated network of buildings anchored around a centralized park. The ground floor of each new building is activated by amenities shared by a campus-wide network. Restaurants, day care facilities, and fitness centers are brought together through a generous landscape outfitted to maximize both interpersonal and digital collaboration.

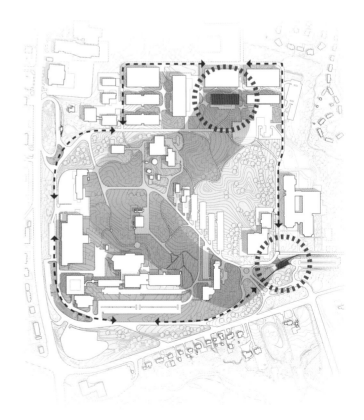

Defining an Entry Experience
One of three new entrances,
the Visitor Reception Building
is a defined threshold into the
campus network. The building is
shaped by a sequence of formal
movements that emerges from
and activates the surrounding
campus landscape.

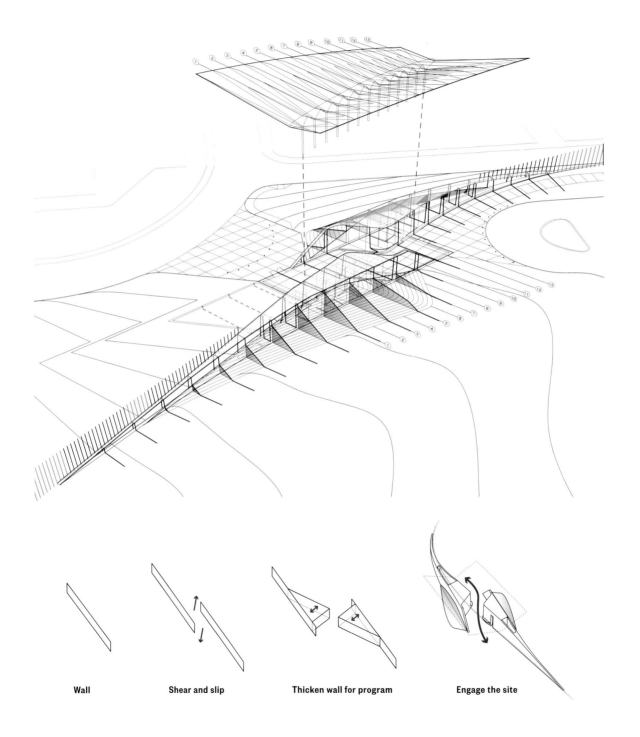

Wall   Shear and slip   Thicken wall for program   Engage the site

A dynamic new gateway to the campus, the Visitor Reception Building is both the public face of the headquarters and an intimately scaled threshold into the campus network. The Visitor Reception provides a legible point of arrival, creating an interface between public and private, landscape and architecture.

The building appears to emerge from the earth, slipping laterally into the campus's perimeter fence to provide a secure, yet permeable passage to receive guests. Entering from an arrival garden, visitors pass into the building through a sequence of open reception, orientation, and gathering spaces beneath a split wing roof canopy that vaults above an enclosure of structural glass. A light-filled box perched below a soaring sculptural roof, the pavilion maximizes natural illumination while capturing bucolic views. From there, a shuttle runs a connective loop through the campus, unifying the pedestrian landscape.

The Visitor Reception Building is an
active participant in the life of the
campus, providing a model of exemplary
environmental performance. The
building is powered by a solar panel
array nestled in the adjacent landscape,
and its sculptural roof acts as a funnel
for rainwater collection.

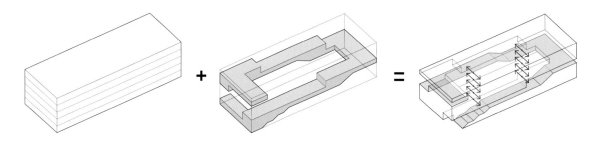

Offices in Open Plan
Open offices provide a flexible, easily reconfigured work environment to maximize daylight and enhance communication.

Communal Living Rooms
Continuous circulation along the building perimeter encourages collaboration at every level.

Flexible Office Environment
Increased visibility between floors, office spaces, and gathering areas creates unique settings for meetings and collaborations.

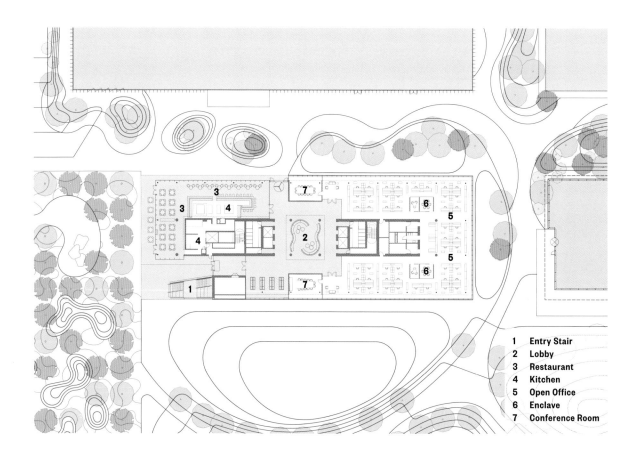

1   Entry Stair
2   Lobby
3   Restaurant
4   Kitchen
5   Open Office
6   Enclave
7   Conference Room

Reimagining the paradigm of the building as a box, the new Oncology Office Building internalizes a shared sense of intimacy and flexibility to create a collaborative work environment. The one-hundred-forty-thousand-square-foot home for Novartis's global oncology offices unfolds over five floors of open office work areas connected by "living rooms" with continuous vistas to the campus. The building draws in the adjacent landscape by "carving out" an ascending spiral of public spaces that climbs upward along the building perimeter, inside and out, as gathering spaces and balconies.

Marked by wood screens, column-free spans, and low-iron glass, the living rooms provide a clear and continuous space for formal, informal, and spontaneous collaborations, facilitating a fluid exchange of ideas. Furnished with custom wingspan chairs that bring tactility and definition to double-height spaces, these living rooms serve to domesticate the office building typology and introduce an alternative spatial rhythm to the workplace, providing a range of microenvironments for spontaneous encounters. The workplace is organized to facilitate evolving operations in which team size and composition vary over time, necessitating a field of easily reconfigurable workstations for the 350-person workforce. Fully-glazed interior conference rooms and smaller enclave spaces allow for privacy within the open layout without disconnecting occupants from the activity of the floor.

This layering of visual impressions across the interior finds its companion in the building exterior, which is composed of three types of glass—acid-etched, reflective, and fritted—to produce a subtle patterned effect, alternately reflective and transparent across the facade that tactically enlivens the crisp rectilinear mass. The placement of the building at the campus's Town Square facilitates connectivity to both the landscape and the neighboring office buildings, allowing for occupants from multiple sectors within the campus to gather in a new collaborative working environment.

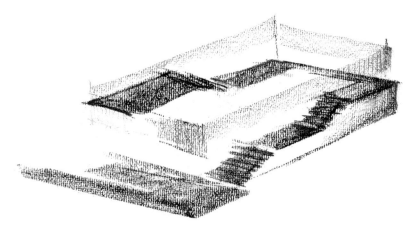

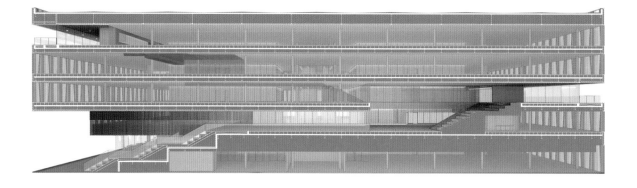

Within the larger volume of the
living room, Weiss/Manfredi's
custom-designed high-back
wingspan chairs create a space-
within-a-space. The folding form
of the chair adds an organic,
playful dimension to the clear and
rational space. Custom-designed
carpets offer tactile warmth to
the open lofts.

To achieve the column-free expression of the double-height living rooms, the upper floors are suspended over the ascending public zone from one hundred-foot-long (30 m) plate girders at the roof, which are cantilevered thirty feet (9 m) from the two central building cores.

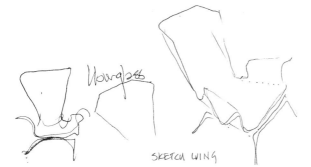

Fifth Level

Open office workspaces
surround the public living rooms.
Centralized building cores
allow for all workstations to be
located within thirty feet (9 m)
of the exterior facade to supply
natural daylight and views to
all occupants.

Fourth Level

Third Level

Second Level

1	Entry Stair
2	Lobby
3	Open Office
4	Enclave
5	Conference Room
6	Living Room
7	Pantry
8	Terrace

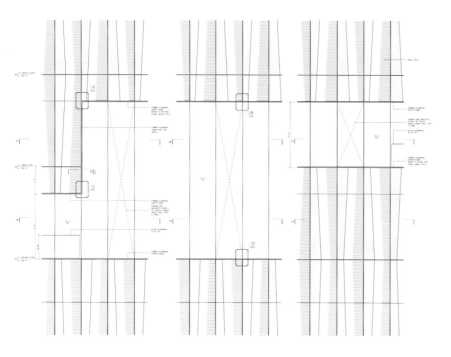

The reflective nature of the facade produces a chameleon-like effect, translating the chroma of the surrounding environments onto the building.

Cornell NYC Tech Co-Location Building

New York, New York

A narrow strip of land in the waters separating Manhattan and Queens, Roosevelt Island has long served as an incubator site for visionary design proposals and utopian speculations. Named Welfare Island for a time, prior to 1973, the island also maintains a mixed history of social experiments, from a penitentiary hospital and lunatic asylum in its earliest days to the distributed school system of the 1969 master plan by Johnson and Burgee. That plan's minimization of automobile traffic and the subsequent introduction of a subsurface pneumatic waste removal system have further contributed to the island's unique and innovative character.

Today, a new vision for the southern end of the island is unfolding, fusing entrepreneurial and academic ambitions within the form of a research campus. New York City has partnered with Cornell University and Israel's Technion University to create "Cornell Tech," a pioneering research initiative aimed at recasting New York as a global technology hub. This two-million-square-foot island incubator is intended to forge vital connections between industry and academia, while simultaneously defining Roosevelt Island as a more engaging urban center woven within metropolitan New York.

The Co-Location Building is shaped by a larger urban context, oriented to frame extraordinary views of the Queensboro Bridge and Manhattan's landmark skyline.

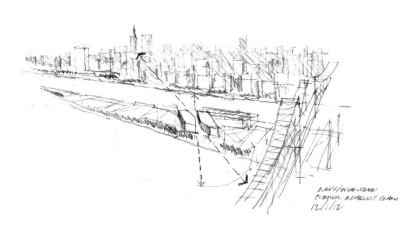

The idea of the research campus is currently undergoing a significant transformation across the globe as universities and private companies are uniting in new ways to foster the development of applied research. This convergence demands a fresh approach to the complex spatial and functional needs of the contemporary research center. Countering the trends of the recent past where corporations fled from cities into exurban parklands, today's campus projects are located in or near major urban centers so as to take advantage of the cultural amenities and transportation services key to attracting and retaining talent.

In acknowledging a healthy reciprocity between innovative research and the urban environment, the planning and design of the contemporary campus is an opportunity to forge a bond across a diverse range of constituents, institutional actors, programs, and scales of inhabitation. As the first Co-Location center on the Roosevelt Island campus, the building defines a new programmatic typology in which academic researchers and professional start-ups share the same space. The building's crystalline geometries frame river-to-river views and bring daylight into all the spaces of the building.

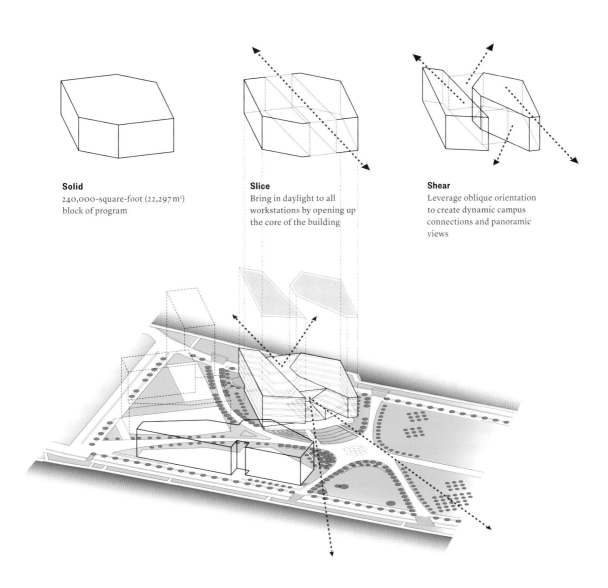

Solid
240,000-square-foot (22,297 m²)
block of program

Slice
Bring in daylight to all
workstations by opening up
the core of the building

Shear
Leverage oblique orientation
to create dynamic campus
connections and panoramic
views

Intended as an incubator of applied research, the Co-Location Building is designed to support a social and technological ecology that breaks down the institutional boundaries to collaborative research, hosting a dialogue between Cornell's three disciplinary hubs: Connective Media, Healthier Life, and the Built Environment. The six-story Co-Location Building is structured internally around a public Tech Gallery flanked by a series of loft-like workspaces, and is shaped by a sequence of formal alignments that activate the surrounding campus landscapes, create connections to the First Academic Building by Morphosis, and frame views across the island.

This ascending central core serves as the social nexus of the building and provides a flexible array of collaborative meeting spaces to support cross-disciplinary interaction. The workspaces themselves continue in this direction, offering an open-plan layout capable of accommodating individual researchers, software developers, start-ups, and large-scale R&D project teams alike. Informed by recent developments in office design that have seen major tech companies such as Google occupy buildings with large expanses of flexible, open floor space, the Co-Location Building is designed to supply an infrastructure for research without limiting its operations to a rigid, fixed spatial configuration. Indoor and outdoor gathering spaces at the ground level of the building plug into the exterior landscape of the Tech Walk, encouraging public programming and education.

Peripheral vision and critical adjacencies throughout the public core and loftlike work spaces support an ecosystem of professional and academic collaboration. Here, movement and continuities shape the architecture to promote circulation through the building's length and out into the landscape.

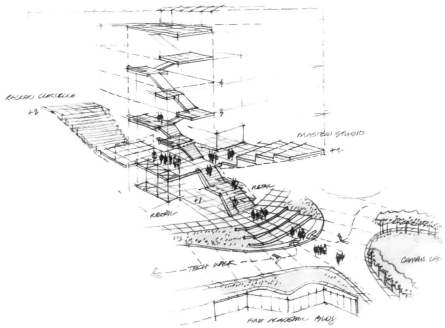

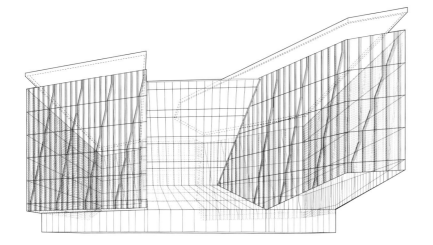

Envelope
A high-performance curtain wall subtly reflects and reveals the structure behind. Two unique types of glass differentiate between the wings of the building and its transparent center.

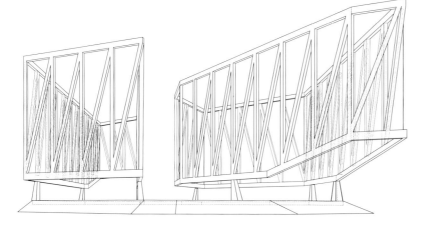

Structure
Five-story-tall steel trusses support two eighty-foot (24 m) cantilevers inspired by the structure of the Queensboro Bridge.

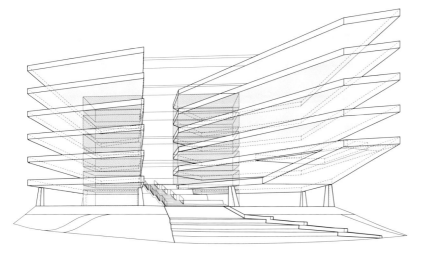

Floor Plates
A split floor plate allows daylight to reach the center of the building, activating its core.

The cantilevered southwest and northeast wings shelter outdoor social spaces that animate the ground floor retail spaces and entry terrace. The silhouette of a rooftop photovoltaic canopy unifies the campus' architectural expression and is an iconic signature of Cornell's commitment to sustainability. Anticipating a new phase of public-private collaboration, the Cornell Tech campus adds another chapter to Roosevelt Island's legacy of experimentation, one that exceeds the confines of site and offers to transform the relationship between work and study, physical and digital, the productive and the social.

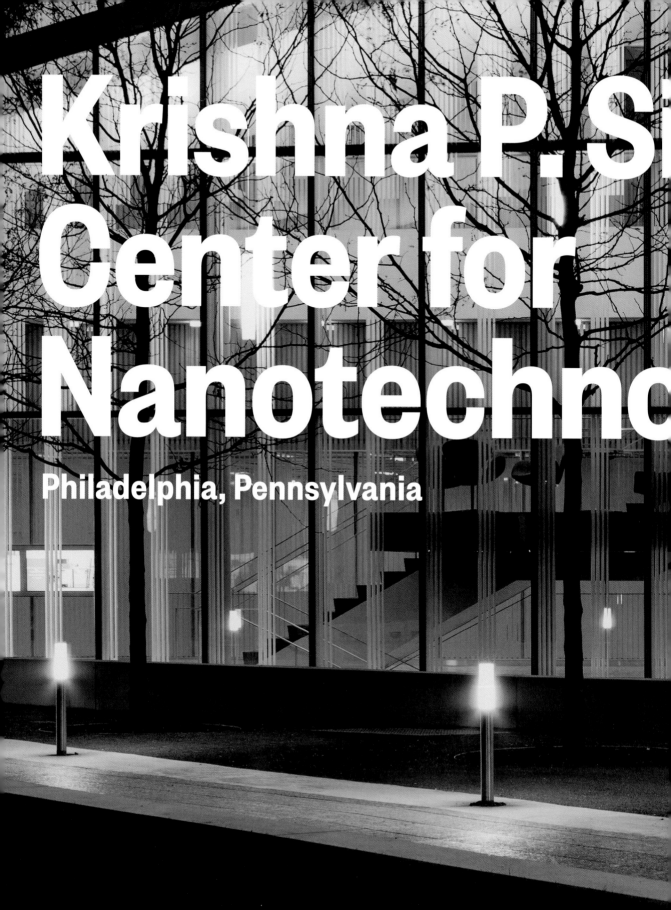

Krishna P. Si Center for Nanotechno

Philadelphia, Pennsylvania

In a ten-thousand-square-foot cleanroom at the Krishna P. Singh Center for Nanotechnology, "bunny" suited researchers from the University of Pennsylvania perform experiments made visible through a UV-resistant amber glass wall to students passing through the adjacent entry galleria. Situated between the labs and exterior enclosure, this public galleria, with video screens illuminating microscopic images from the researchers' equipment, acts as a public lens that reveals the scientists' emerging research. Across the galleria, researchers gather on inhabitable glass and granite stairs that initiate an interior topography that ascends to a public forum cantilevering sixty-eight feet over the building's landscaped forecourt. There, a cubic Tony Smith sculpture stands in relief to the transparent structure spiraling around the site perimeter.

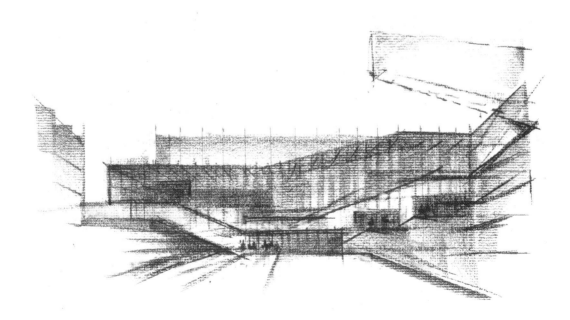

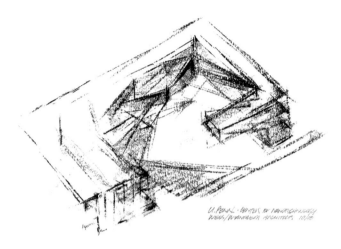

Both the University of
Pennsylvania and the city of
Philadelphia have a tradition
of organizing buildings around
open quads. The Singh Center
simultaneously presents a new
campus green and gateway
identity at the urban edge of
the institution.

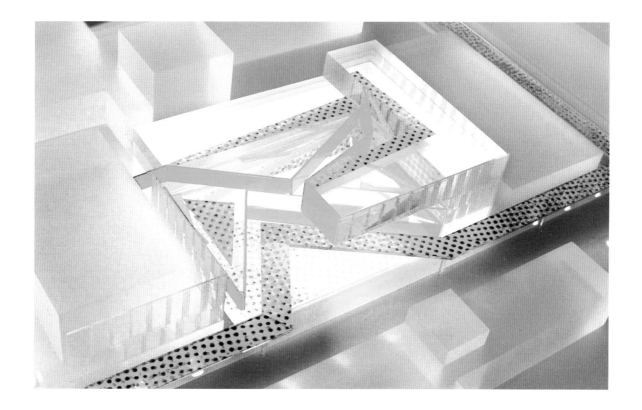

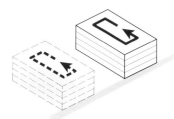

Conventional lab box

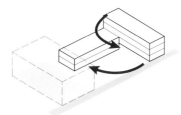

Unhinging the box

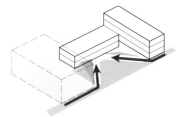

Folding landscape

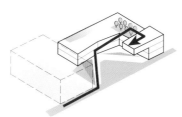

Circulation helix

Laboratory buildings are typically organized around a central corridor and afford little public space. The Center for Nanotechnology inverts this model, focusing the laboratories around a central quad, opening the sciences to the university landscape, and making research activities highly visible.

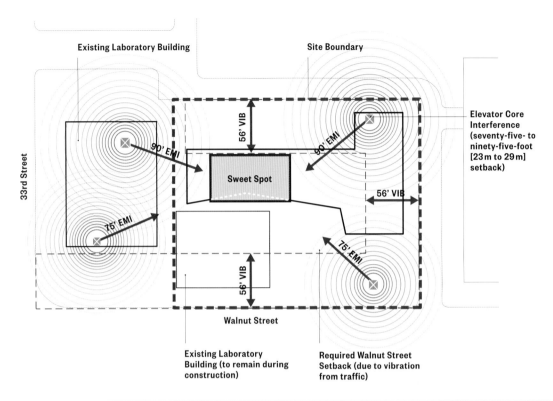

Existing Laboratory Building

Site Boundary

Elevator Core
Interference
(seventy-five- to
ninety-five-foot
[23 m to 29 m]
setback)

56' VIB

90' EMI

90' EMI

Sweet Spot

56' VIB

33rd Street

75' EMI

75' EMI

56' VIB

Walnut Street

Existing Laboratory
Building (to remain during
construction)

Required Walnut Street
Setback (due to vibration
from traffic)

Sweet
Spot

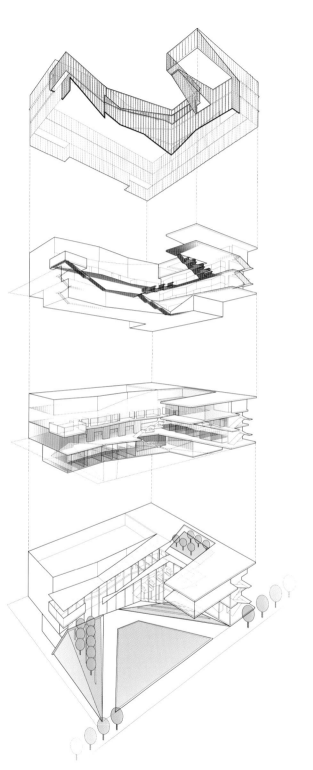

Skin
Glass Curtain Wall
Metal Panel

Circulation
Primary Route
Secondary Route

Research and Collaboration
Forum Space
Offices
Clean Room
Characterization Suite
General Laboratories

Landscape
Green Roof
Campus Landscape

Defining the "Sweet Spot"
More sensitive research is
conducted below grade within
a sweet spot removed from
electromagnetic interference and
environmental contaminants,
such as noise and vibration. The
building is set back from the street,
and elevator and utility cores
are displaced to the perimeter
of the building to create a
dedicated research zone at the
heart of the project.

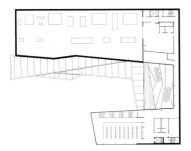

Third Level

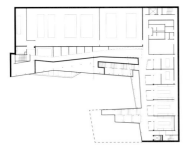

Second Level

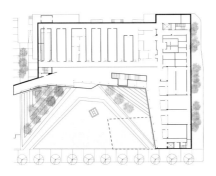

First Level

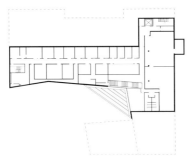

Lower Level

Nanoscale research is at the core of radical break-throughs that transcend disciplinary boundaries of engineering, medicine, and the sciences. The Singh Center marks the university's first cross-disciplinary building between the sciences and engineering, and was designed to further the col-laborative ambitions driving the project. Scientific research facilities are usually consigned to remote areas within conventional campus plans, or, if located in an urban context, they are entombed within fortress-like containers in order to protect the sensitive equipment that advanced research requires. The site for the Singh Center places the building at the northeast corner of the University's West Philadelphia campus, making it the first campus building encountered by those arriving from downtown Philadelphia along Walnut Street.

Embracing the site's position at the hinge of two distinct urban areas, the building is designed to both mark the transition from city to campus and to serve as a public showcase for innovative research, which all too often goes unseen. By plac-ing the research on display, the inward-oriented focus of a traditional research facility is inverted. Simultaneously, researchers are relieved of their usual isolation through the introduction of as much natural light as possible into the lab spaces and shared amenities, such as conference rooms and lounge spaces, all visually connected throughout the building.

Though restrictive, the complex technical
parameters of the laboratory program enhance the
building's architectural and urban potential. Visual
and physical connections are introduced throughout the building to promote interaction between
scientists and engineers. Externally, the laboratory
defines a new campus green as a microcosm of
Penn's famed Quadrangle.

Light-Sensitive Clean Room

Amber Glass Filter

Public Galleria

General Lab

Exposing the Research

The most sensitive nanotechnology research requires complete
isolation from vibration and
ultraviolet light waves. In the
clean room, amber-colored glass
filters ultraviolet light to protect
photosensitive nanofabrication
equipment inside the labs,
allowing the public to view the
research from the building's
public galleria.

The clean room is the functional core of the Singh Center, strategically centralized at its front door. The clean room is designed in a flexible bay-and-chase configuration to accommodate multiple research processes. Bays provide for the individualization of clean room process spaces, and chases provide space for support equipment.

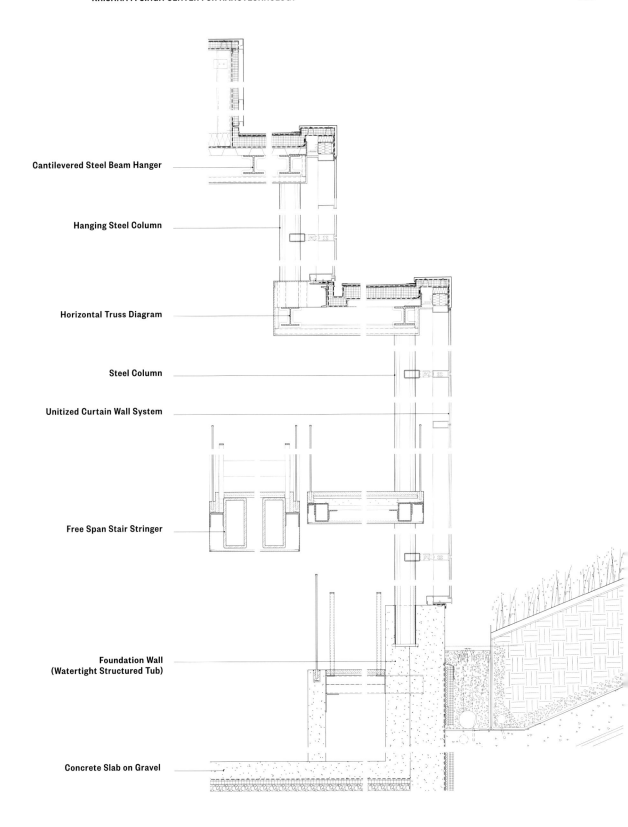

Cantilevered Steel Beam Hanger

Hanging Steel Column

Horizontal Truss Diagram

Steel Column

Unitized Curtain Wall System

Free Span Stair Stringer

Foundation Wall
(Watertight Structured Tub)

Concrete Slab on Gravel

Cantilevered Forum
The building's spatial sequence spirals upward, unfurling around the courtyard to culminate in a dramatic cantilever. Inside, a multipurpose forum provides a setting for lectures, meetings, and events with a panoramic view toward the heart of Penn's campus.

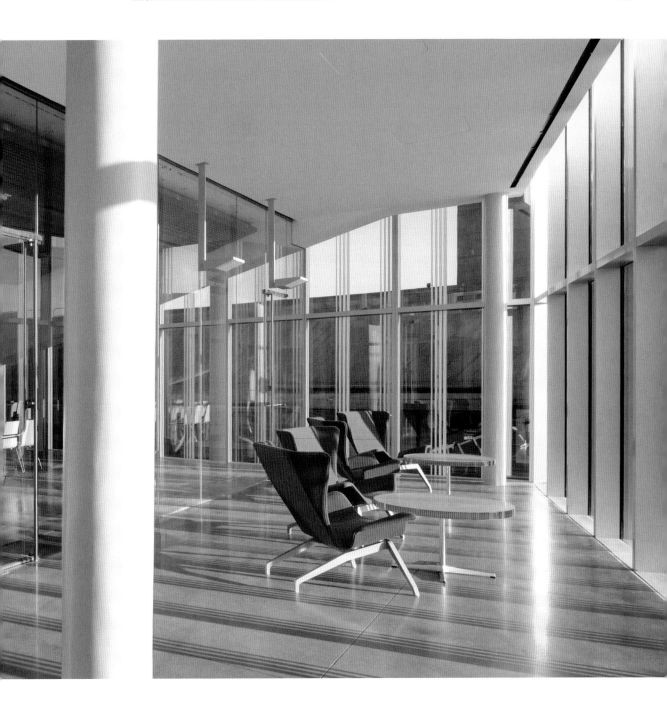

The open courtyard offers an inviting outpost at the edge of the expanding urban campus. Cutting across the courtyard, two paved pathways frame an oblique approach to the building entrance. This oblique approach initiates a visual and physical sequence of circulation through the building that precludes any sense of static resolution. The tightly woven sequence finally ascends to an apex of public destinations, where the roof garden and cantilevered forum opens to panoramic views of the historic heart of Penn's campus. From the nano to the urban and from individual researcher to interdisciplinary collaboration, the Singh Center choreographs a complex interplay of scales with an unfolding origami of precise formal and social relationships.

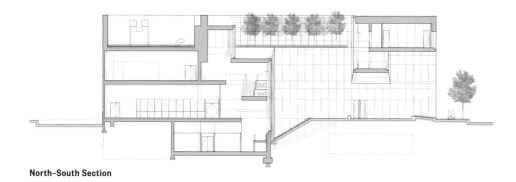

North–South Section

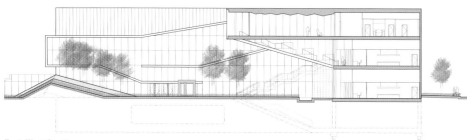

East–West Section

The facade and ceiling of the galleria slip and fold to create a column-free gathering space. Spiraling upward to the building's peak, the visual signature of the cantilever springs sixty-eight feet (21m) beyond the building's structure below.

Lateral Connecting Truss
- Creates column-free galleria
- Provides stability, resists wind loads, and provides sun shade
- Columns above are suspended in tension from a cantilevered beam; columns below act in compression

Inverted Truss Cantilever
Sixty-eight-foot (21m) structural
cantilever supports a suspended
column structure and hung floor
truss

This new campus quad hosts two green roofs and a water storage tank under the central green. A public living roof has native plantings and creates a synthetic relationship to the courtyard below. The rooftop mechanical areaway is planted with sedum and succulents.

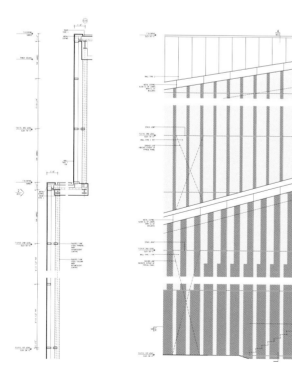

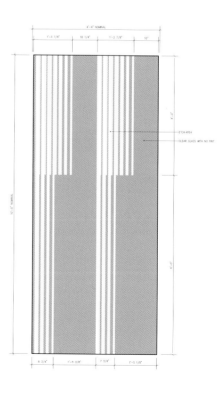

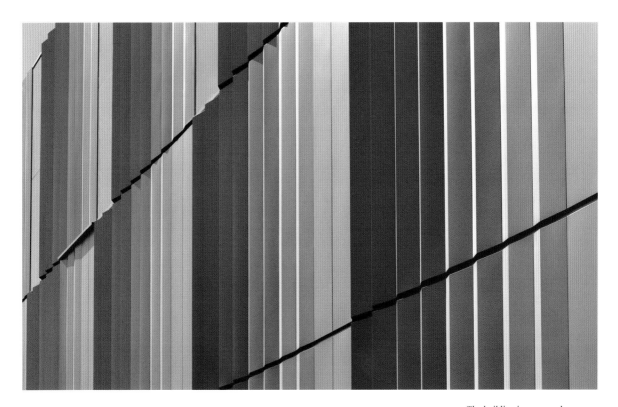

The building is expressed materially through a syncopated facade of glass and aluminum panels. The glazing is oriented around the central quad to bring light and views into all lab and office spaces. Pleated metal panels create an opaque facade at specialized labs and mechanical spaces.

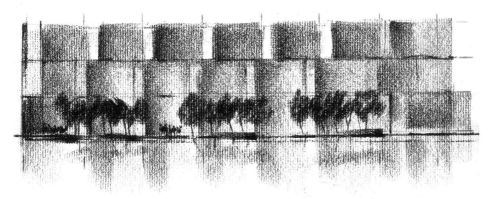

Megaform and Public Natures

Kenneth Frampton
Marion Weiss
Michael A. Manfredi
Justin Fowler

Megaform and Public Natures

**Kenneth Frampton | Marion Weiss |
Michael A. Manfredi | Justin Fowler**

First published in 1999, Kenneth Frampton's "Megaform as Urban Landscape" articulated a need for delimited large-scale interventions within the incoherent placelessness of the neoliberal megalopolis. Equal parts historical survey and projective manifesto, Frampton's tome suggested that an architecture of resistance would take on a unitary formal character verging on the topographic. Following Hannah Arendt's notion of the "space of public appearance," such projects would exhibit the qualities of a landmark while also promoting civic life within the city through an engagement with hybrid programming. Writing in a discursive moment where discussions of "bigness," "shape," "datascape," and "iconicity" were poised to give way to the systemic and pedagogical leviathan of "landscape urbanism," Frampton offered a narrative of an unknown quantity brought about through a fidelity to tectonic firmness—hope for the achievement of poetic surplus through an attention to the demands of necessity. Over a decade since that initial shot across the bow, Frampton continues revising and expanding his arsenal of exemplary forms as an anxious fortification of an argument that appears, perhaps by design, to be perpetually incomplete.

To continue the discussion in contemporary terms, Frampton sat down with Marion Weiss, Michael Manfredi, and Justin Fowler to discuss the future of the remedial mega-project and its place within the built-out urban centers of today's cities. The conversation followed a series of continuous studio investigations entitled "Evolutionary Infrastructures," conducted by Marion Weiss and Michael Manfredi at the University of Pennsylvania and the

Harvard Graduate School of Design. The investigation sought
to reenvision complex urban thresholds, layered with complex
interplays of constructed and natural systems, testing the potential
of an evolutionary, inhabitable, and hybrid form of infrastructure
—a new megaform. One such site focused on the highway corridor
spanning from the George Washington Bridge to the Alexander
Hamilton Bridge in Upper Manhattan—an armature described by
Reyner Banham in his 1976 book, *Megastructure*, as "the largest and
most visually convincing of all accidental megastructures."[1]

Nearly four decades after Banham's eulogy for the megastructure, this infrastructural found object, with its Pier Luigi
Nervi–designed bus terminal and highway-straddling housing slabs
from the mid-1960s, remains a functioning yet underperforming
urban complex. This conversation takes the site investigation
as a starting point to address the evolution of the architectural
mega-project.

Marion Weiss: The term "evolutionary infrastructures" was intended
to invoke a more open-ended understanding of what a megaform
might be, particularly as it relates to systemic operations that
are either embedded (a part of) or invented for (on behalf of) a
territory like this. We have a suspicion that the megaform is not yet
doing enough work. The section is not quite holding up its end of
the bargain and infrastructures remain too monofunctional. As it
relates to our academic investigations, the real question was, what
would we add or take away if we were to somehow re-engage fifty
years later the potential promise of the visions that were never realized? It's right by a park, it's near the water, and it's embedded within
the city, which is unusual, since most of these strange concoctions
are always on the edges. So what would we do? And that's one of
the questions of our transformative intervention position. But the
other one asks, is there anything prototypically compelling about
the situation—and the situational change over time—that we might
invoke in some other parts of the world?

Michael Manfredi: Frampton's "Megaform" also offered a valuable
lens to focus our investigation. What interested us in the shift from
"megastructure" (Banham's term via Maki) into "megaform" was the

emphasis on the horizontal and topographic character of the projects. We also wanted to introduce into this conversation a means by which to systematically pursue an ecological agenda. Given the imperatives of connectivity and the implication of operating at a mega-scale, we could privilege ecological systems and energy patterns in a more holistic way. We are also drawn to the hybrid, programmatic capacity of the megaform and its potential for an embedded public presence. By sheer virtue of size, multiple public and private programs could coexist and function simultaneously.

Justin Fowler: What was it that drew you to this site and how did you see it relating to today?

MW: We were certainly seduced by this strange assemblage of pieces that amounted to a de facto megastructure. Taken piece by piece, there are moments of real architectural quality. Nervi's George Washington Bridge bus terminal is exemplary, but even the four housing towers have a kind of power in their seriality. There's also the fact that this project remains something of a curiosity in Manhattan; a place one often passes through by car on the way to somewhere else. At the regional scale, it's a piece of transit infrastructure, yet for the neighborhood of Washington Heights, it's a home for thousands of people. Banham understood this project as a megastructure, yet it was a piecemeal utopia particular in many ways to the American context.

MM: The Port Authority of New York owned the land, so the project was actually one of the first major public-private initiatives in this country, utilizing air-rights development transfers to support housing for displaced residents above the expressway. The project was not only radical as an economic model, it also embodied ambitions of merging infrastructural and architectural ambitions. The Nervi bus terminal is an extraordinary combination of structural bravura and passive mechanical venting of bus exhaust, and the Bridge Apartments, although architecturally less distinguished, were the country's first large-scale use of lightweight aluminum facades. In fact, the initial design for the towers included elements to reduce noise and air pollution, although these elements were sadly never included in the completed towers.

MW: The initial success of this project—or at least its demonstration of the feasibility of working at the infrastructural scale within the city—led the Ford Foundation to sponsor the study that produced Paul Rudolph's now infamous project for the Lower Manhattan Expressway. The idea of "measuring utopia," which was the subtitle of the Harvard studio investigation in 2011, came from this disjunction between image and political reality. Why was the Rudolph scheme seen as provocative and utopian if the project in Washington Heights actually teased out the complex contingencies at play in bringing a megastructure to fruition? We wanted to investigate the familiar images of classic megastructures in order to suggest that the history is not as tidy as we might now believe. All of this became an interesting trigger for us to take stock of this site some fifty years later to consider how its formal, material, and economic legacies might serve as a point of departure for considering the future of large-scale remedial transformations in the city.

Kenneth Frampton: If one were to turn my "Megaform" lecture into a real book, it would need a lot of work in terms of adding other examples, but would also need to define how the idea of a megaform could be interpreted as a realistic strategy. In 1999 a task force headed up by Richard Rogers produced a paper entitled, "Towards an Urban Renaissance." The group's primary task was to anticipate the building needs for the United Kingdom over the next twenty years (from 2000 to 2020). Some smart aleck on the team wrote that one has to accept that 90 percent of what will exist in the year 2020 has already been built. I find that statement to be a really terrific rhetorical game and I've no doubt that it's right. The proliferation of freestanding objects in the megalopolis ad infinitum makes it nearly impossible to negotiate the whole urban environment without the aid of graphic signs. There are so few genuine landmarks. With the arrival of portable GPS devices and smartphones, perhaps this is less of an issue, but nevertheless, the contrary role of the landmark can hardly be considered obsolete. That aspect of the megaform—megaform as landmark—would be one of its virtues as a critical intervention in the urban environment.

MW: And landmark has to be distinct from icon?

KF: You could say landform as well, perhaps. What's important is the horizontal continuity of the form and that it's recognizable as such, and also understandable as such, meaning outside you can see it and inside you can experience it. It is a sort of compensatory project, which compensates for the privatization of the mega-lopolis, as compared to the balance of public and private found in traditional urbanism. I think it was Jean Nouvel who said, rhetori-cally of course, that urbanism is no longer possible, period. It's gone, it's over. I suppose what he has in mind is so-called tradi-tional urbanism. And, honestly, where historical cities are still in place—which would include Philadelphia, despite people's best efforts to destroy it—you can still operate within an identifiable urban fabric that has a public aspect. Once one is out of this, into the megalopolis, then it's all privatized—it's like the provisional title of Wright's 1932 book on the city, *The Disappearing City*. What I've just been saying is not very well articulated inside the "Megaform" document. I don't find it very easy to unpack the current situation.

I would hesitate to put the emphasis entirely on "infrastruc-ture." It is key of course, and you could say that some of the projects illustrated in "Megaform" take infrastructure as the primary driver of the form. Look at Le Corbusier's incredible intuition with his project for Algiers. And then you have the pathos of the Smithsons' London Roads Study, much later on, where they also realize that the permanent civil engineering operation is to receive the auto-mobile. With Corbusier, because he's so intuitive and intelligent, he realizes very early on that infrastructure is a very strong aspect of the emerging reality and tries to capitalize on that. It's incredible when you see the perspective of it; the roadway is in the middle of the block. And then he stacks into the framework all these Spanish colonial houses and any old stylistic kitsch you want. I find it incredible he would do that, because he recognizes, after all, that it doesn't really matter if you load the frame with stuff because the frame will have such a big presence at this scale that the trivial kitsch wouldn't matter. That's obviously what he understands. But at the same time it's very utopian—well, we didn't build it, did we?

MW: No, although the Pedregulho social housing project in Brazil pulled off something within earshot of Corbusier's vision. Affonso Reidy built a slice of that larger figure around the topographic edge of the site.

KF: But he didn't make it into a road; it just imitates the form of an infrastructural spine. The inherent problem with the autoroute, however, is that it is a processual extrusion. Le Corbusier was the first who recognized that, to a greater extent than the railway, it constitutes a new geography; a kind of artificial ground upon which one could build. This is the obsessive vision leading from the first sketches for Rio of 1929 to the Plan Obus for Algiers of 1930. Despite the fact that the car seems to be quite literally at one's doorstep, it is not so easy to access the multistory block above the roadway. I think there is a lot to be said for dense hybrid structures that are served by the autoroute system; however such structures don't have to be built directly over the route. The L'Illa block in Barcelona is built to one side of the Avenida Diagonal and not over it. This is an argument I attempt to advance with the idea of megaform; a concept inspired by the L'Illa block.

JF: At the moment, there appears to be an uneasy alliance between your project of megaform and perhaps the more infrastructural project of landscape urbanism, which seem tenuously united beneath an umbrella aesthetic of the "topographic." In many respects the formal manifestation of landscape urbanist projects is a didactic transposition of the systemic processes at work (suggesting a one-to-one correspondence between an economy

Pedregulho social housing, by Affonso Eduardo Reidy, Rio de Janeiro, 1952

L'Illa Diagonal, by Rafael Moneo and Manuel de Solà-Morales, Barcelona, 1993

of performance and expression), yet the megaform is buttressed by
your advocacy for the "tectonic," which has both a rational material logic, but also a surplus poetic effect or some sort of irreducible
element. How would you characterize the relation between the
ecological ambitions of landscape urbanism and the formal drive of
the megaform? Is there a rigid economy in the former that might act
as a detriment to the symbolic or placemaking quality of the latter?

KF: If you accept that it's a question of remedial strategy, then—and
I feel this very strongly—architects have more to learn from intelligent landscape architects than the other way around. I particularly
admire Michel Desvigne and the landscape school in Versailles
founded by his mentor, Michel Corajoud, but what do we actually know about it? We have schools of architecture, we encourage
people to do research, and yet all over the place there is material
that no one ever touches. Two things come to mind—one is that
landscape school and the other is Curitiba. Everyone knows about
Curitiba, Brazil, but we know nothing. Jaime Lerner was mayor
there for fifteen years, and I was struck by a line from a lecture of
his where he said, "as a figure of power, I have to work fast to defeat
my own bureaucracy." This attitude has a certain relevance in the
context of the megaform discussion. We desperately need to expand
our frame of reference and absorb some of the lessons from these
situations, particularly as it relates to strategies of implementation.

If we come back to landscape urbanism and this question of
megaform as urban landscape, I think I know the kind of work that
Charles Waldheim has done, and also James Corner, and again we

Olympic Sculpture Park,
by Weiss/Manfredi, Seattle,
Washington, 2007

come back to "know" and "don't know." Waldheim has pushed
landscape urbanism as a didactic framework, but one really has to
work at it to tease out the substance. It is clear, however, that they're
productively engaging with the idea of remedial operations in a
megalopolis that is already built-out.

MW: There does, however, seem to be an antipathy toward architectural form that's intrinsic to the remedial project.

KF: It doesn't have to be that way. What you did with the Seattle
Olympic Sculpture Park provides a necessary kind of architectural
gesture, but through the material of large-scale earth manipulation. It's a sort of extraordinary thing you've produced, breathtaking
from so many points of view, and it's also an achievement vis-à-vis
infrastructure. It repairs a rift and brings people from the city to the
water. This is landscape urbanism, but as is true in this profession
in general, given that techno-science rules the world, these kinds
of humanist fields have always looked to legitimize themselves by
evoking techno-science. What is interesting about architecture is
that it's a very quixotic and durable practice. It remains at this crucial
interface where it cannot simply be reasoned away. Architecture
touches reality like no other profession.

JF: To continue along this thread on the human aspect of the architectural endeavor, one of the striking things about your position is
that the megaform requires a decisive authorial stroke across the
urban fabric. In many respects, this kind of language is not at all
dissimilar from Robert Somol's defense of the "shape" or "logo"
project. I'm thinking specifically here of his line that, "neither natural
nor necessary, the graphic can only be artificially asserted and
subsequently played out."[2] This statement leads me to believe that
the distinction between megaform and shape, or even "bigness" is
less a formal one and more about the kinds of political values that
underwrite their respective "assertions." Clearly, there's as much
topographic manipulation in a large-scale project by BIG or MVRDV
as there is in the most exemplary urban work of Moneo or Steven
Holl, so the difference might require some articulation in terms of
values beyond form. Given that there seems to be an urgent appeal

to political necessity in your [Frampton's] work, how would you characterize this dimension of the megaform project as it relates to the
issue of shape?

KF: There are two words that I think the architectural profession
was somewhat uneasy about for a long period of time. One is
"beauty" and the other is "form." And for me, too, if you look at
what I've written, form doesn't feature that prominently. Given
my personal history, I realized the importance of form rather
late in the game. But this question of form and image; you can't
dismiss this question.

But I think what you're saying is very important, which is
this issue of necessity. I am very prejudiced about this. I think, for
example, that inside many contemporary buildings there is nothing;
literally nothing, because their architects are not interested at
all in what's in the buildings. Whatever the program is, they just
stuff it in there. All they're interested in is the shape and the surface.
I'm being very prejudicial, but I think I'm right. And the question
of what is the space, and what is the program of the space—what
is inside the building—is crucial, I think. That doesn't mean
that the form/image issue is not important. If one is going to invoke
landmark, obviously form and image are of consequence. That's
why I think this step formation of L'Illa Diagonal by Moneo and
de Solà-Morales gives the block a character or profile that is identifiable, and that's important. One could say the same about Alvar
Aalto's Baker Dormitory at MIT.

MW: You're getting to the issue of silhouette and symbolism, too.
The silhouette of Jørn Utzon's Opera House in Sydney is a case where
the wild perimeter of the water's edge heaves up into something
that's highly legible, almost a landform more than a building on the
edge of the land.

KF: It's undeniable that the Sydney Opera House became a symbol
of Australia as well as a symbol of Sydney, like the Eiffel Tower in
a way. And how do you compete with the Sydney Harbor Bridge? It
was a big thing to answer to that bridge.

MW: It's a consequence of the public datum.

KF: And the approach, it's like an Acropolis approach.

MM: Right, and as with the Acropolis, if you took the ground plane away from the Opera House, it would be much diminished and much less interesting. With the Opera House, the ground plane, though relatively contained, is as crucial as the silhouette. The variegated series of peninsulas that define the Sydney harbor are translated by Utzon into a strong topographic form where distinctions between the ground plane and the harbor walk are ambiguous except where they converge at the plinth, or datum, from which the signature silhouette of the roofs emerge.

KF: But then you have to ask the question: Why don't they build just one Opera House, why did they have to build two? There you come back to the importance of programmatic issues.

MM: But the beauty of the two is like the twinning of the former World Trade Center. Sometimes you see it as one, and at other times you see the pair. This pairing provides a kind of urban compass or gyroscope and way of understanding your geographic orientation.

KF: It comes back to good architects and the difficulty in being a good architect; of imagining the program and imagining the work are equally charged. The program is crucial.

Sydney Opera House, by
Jørn Utzon, Sydney, 1973

MW: Lately, we've been preoccupied with this notion of sequence and section and the belief that these are things that start to temper or catalyze the legitimacy of a megaform or megastructure particularly as it relates to a larger urban scale. This potential is part of what we were teasing out in the Evolutionary Infrastructures studio investigations—this sense that something larger is at stake. Something larger is at stake politically and materially because a whole host of systems seem to be completely in conflict with one another—at the Trans Manhattan expressway site, for instance, the improbable juxtaposition of an expressway cutting through the city with thirty-two-story towers spanning ten lanes of traffic raises the question of what additions and transformations need to be introduced to create common ground within these seemingly incompatible systems.

MM: At the same time, the image of the figure and its scale remain important. Because you can see the towers from as far away as Central Park, you can begin to understand their relationship to the city: their east/west deployment marks the route of the highway, yet each tower is rotated north/south to mark the predominant grain of the grid.

KF: There's this beautiful project of Le Corbusier's for the Paris Exposition of 1937 that consists of four Y-shaped Cartesian skyscrapers that all come to the same height. In the sketch you see he established a new datum by bringing them all to the same height, which is of course the same idea as the Ville Contemporaine. And you could say that the big virtue of these four slabs was that they came to the same height. It's strange how rare this is. A comparable example might be the London County Council's Roehampton Alton Estate project from the 1950s.

MM: Wallace Harrison did something similar with his towers in Albany, albeit for a more civic purpose. Seriality and repetition are played out to amplify this civic effect.

KF: The question is: Does it or does it not establish a new datum, and is that new datum something that could be read visually as a landmark with a certain horizontality as opposed to being a product of

Empire State Plaza, by Wallace
Harrison, Albany, New York, 1976

this open-ended capitalist development where everything is
coming to a different height according to what one can get away
with? And when I made my slightly uncalled-for remarks about
Philadelphia earlier it had to do with this feeling I have, because
when I came to the United States for the first time in 1965, there
wasn't a single high-rise building in Philadelphia. Now when you
visit Philadelphia you think, most of them are so awful, and why
was it that we just couldn't do better than that?

JF: One thing we haven't touched on is who, namely the body
politic, animates this idea of the megaform as a means of resistance. The proliferation of triumphalist narratives of the city, such
as those by Richard Florida and Edward Glaeser, seems to suggest
that cities are primed to receive a new wave of people, both young
and old, who see certain benefits to living in an urban environment.
At the same time, though, the accommodation of this influx appears
to entail reproducing an image of suburban life within city centers
through a kind of amenity urbanism, where what's being offered
in terms of public space does not really challenge the status quo.
From bike lanes to pop-up plazas, so much of what's changing
in New York, for example, is occurring at street level and has yet to
really register an impact on the fundamental form of the city.
   In this context, your concern with Hannah Arendt's distinction between labor and work is particularly interesting because
it speaks to the issue of social character and the need for political
resilience in the face of perceived technological or economic
inevitability. Here, the megaform serves as a proxy in this broader
debate over social values, and in many respects, its remedial aims

are primarily social, since the formal repair of our cities has to be underwritten by a renewed ecological consciousness. David Riesman, whose 1950 book *The Lonely Crowd* arrived in the same decade as Arendt's 1958 *The Human Condition*, understood that issues of consciousness involved work, play, and education, and that the job of remediating consumer culture and its urban by-products would have to take place from within that social space. It seems as though the megaform operates from this realist position and programmatically has adopted both play and education as paths of resistance. What's not entirely clear, however, is the way in which a megaform might intensify or transform the experience of these programs so that there are greater social and formal reverberations. In effect, how does amenity provision graduate into a more substantive public act?

KF: There are some new projects in Hong Kong that offer an interesting take on that challenge. I recently came across the work of architect Rocco Yim, and the interesting thing about the high-rise buildings he's constructed in that incredibly dense city is how they're organized to relieve monotony. For instance, he's designed a twenty-four-story building for the Hong Kong Polytechnic University consisting of a sixteen-story hotel on top of an eight-story teaching facility, but then it's also supposed to be a hotel school. What he does in some of these high-rise buildings is to build into the block, some way up the height of the structure, a breakout space or green space, which consists of a gymnasium or swimming pool or other kinds of amenities.

MW: It acts as a kind of public datum that's not at the level of the street, yet is shared for recreation.

KF: Yes, I find that fascinating. You can say that one of the beautiful aspects of the high-rise type is the tower-like quality, but on the other side, what is somewhat discouraging is the endless repetition of one floor after another. It's an interesting formal and programmatic issue to think through how to begin to create variety within a tall building and how to mediate or transform a group of them through new kinds of spatial linkages.

MW: You're raising an issue about cities that is very important.
In cities we have compressed footprints; we need to move vertically,
and once we move vertically the idea of a datum, which is public
but is not at the street level, becomes fraught—it's privatized
immediately when it's raised, so to what degree do we find public
life and private ties in these secondary datums?

KF: In the 1960s there was a big debate about whether the space
of a mall was public space. This was a debate that took place, if
I remember correctly, at a legal level because of the restrictions
imposed by owners of malls on public discourse in their spaces. And
it was decided, of course, that it isn't public space, but I don't think
that means that one should take an unrealistic attitude toward
the potential socializing benefits of semipublic space in an otherwise commercial space, since it is in some sense a semipublic space
as well. And also, from the point of view of entertainment and
pleasure and other activities, you could say that the provision of
such space remains a strategy that is open to society to compensate
for increasing privatization. The fact is, it's not public in the sense
that the agora is public, but there are still positive opportunities
to be leveraged.

MM: I want to return to this whole idea of the relation between work
and play because we're seeing it transpire in both urban corporate campuses such as Novartis, in Basel, Switzerland, and also in
the urban university settings such as Barnard College in New York
City, where you might bring your food into the library or go to a
coffee shop to study. Everything is commingled in surprising and
interesting ways. If the city is relevant as a place to enjoy a level of
authenticity that you don't get elsewhere, I wonder if the opportunity to bring "authenticity" into semipublic space is also partially a
function of scale and density; where programmatic variety is actually
more possible in big hybrid projects.

    Although there have been moments of consensus in archi-
tectural discourse around the necessity of incremental fine-grain
urban development to promote societal connections, it is productive to consider the mega-scale as a catalyst for social engagement.
We believe the scalar breach between the city structure and the

megastructure might sponsor the emergence of new kinds of public spaces difficult to achieve within more conventional urban or suburban planning models. Intrinsic to this potential alchemy is the recognition that anything that has systemic potential must leverage the tools available to architects, landscape architects, ecologists, and infrastructure engineers.

For instance, with our design for the Olympic Sculpture Park in Seattle, the design is a constructed hybrid—equal parts natural, cultural, infrastructural—reinvented through the lenses of geometry and topography. Our intent was to create an armature that nurtures unexpected uses and activities, but the strength of the project depends on its location within the city.

MW: You can't have intensity without some density, and that's the real issue.

MM: A discovery we stumbled across quite by accident in the context of looking at urban campuses occurred when we went over to the new Google headquarters here in New York, which is located in the city's largest horizontal building, a former Port Authority building. What Google has discovered is that now there are a greater number of employees that want to move from their sylvan suburban campuses in California to that urban location. Perhaps this stems from a need for social interaction, and there may be a glimmer of hope in that. Their workforce is composed of very sophisticated, very international, and technologically savvy employees, yet there is a hunger for some of the "dirt" of the city with its frictions and surprising interactions. The New York City Google headquarters can be described as a default megaform institutionalized as a corporate campus now capable of utilizing the city as an agent of change to its isolated and potentially static identity. In this context, the urban campus can be seen as a program or type uniquely conducive to the characteristics of the megaform.

KF: That situation also has to do with the argument that the spontaneous face-to-face interaction of bright people produces unpredictable results in terms of scientific experiments, and that's a fairly old story, in terms of justifying campuses.

JF: The parkland corporate campus model produced some particularly strong megaforms. Kevin Roche's projects for Union Carbide and Richardson-Vicks in Connecticut, for example, were highly gestural and topographic pieces of infrastructure articulated at the scale of architecture. Each incorporated the space of the automobile very directly into its form, yet the provision of interior common spaces for employees was equally as generous. Positioned outside of an urban fabric, however, these projects don't register as a scalar breach, so it's not entirely clear how they would work within the context of a place like New York City. Here, it will be interesting to witness how research campus mega-projects play out, such as the New York University expansion and the Cornell/Technion venture on Roosevelt Island.

 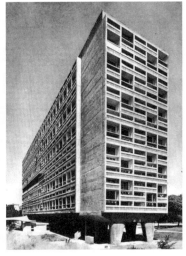

MW: The shape of many contemporary cities has been unduly impacted by the monofunctional demands of transportation infrastructure, or conversely, that of postwar mass housing. Ultimately, what we're trying to arrive at is the question of why such mega-projects are relevant today in the context of existing cities and how they can be retooled to accommodate a high quality of life. If, in a sense, China has already done the sort of thing that was deemed utopian fifty years ago, and they're doing it bigger, faster, wider, and to some degree with very little self-criticism, what's the relevance

Union Carbide Corporate Center, by Kevin Roche John Dinkeloo and Associates, Danbury, Connecticut, 1982

Unité d'Habitation, by Le Corbusier, Marseille, 1952

now in looking more strategically at this question and taking this look so long after its initial historical moment? If you consider ambitious proposals, such as Le Corbusier's 1931 Fort l'Empereur in Algiers, Kenzo Tange's 1960 Tokyo Bay project, and Paul Rudolph's 1967 study for the Lower Manhattan expressway, their promise of a systemic coexistence of infrastructure and inhabitation has still gone largely unfulfilled. Those ambitions were powerful and in some ways more carefully calibrated and crafted compared to what's actually being realized today. So the question that we're really interested in is how do we bring in these older examples in order to think critically about this issue today, and is there something we are taking forward that really can be recast? Terms such as "landform," "megaform," "megastructure," "landscape"—these are all rubrics that have loose-fit overlaps with one another. What's relevant for us now to consider as we go forward?

KF: Clearly Tange's Tokyo Bay of 1960 is a remarkable work, but in the end it derives from Le Corbusier's postwar Unité planning strategy as manifest in his 1945–46 proposal for La Rochelle-Pallice—an anti-suburban model allowing one to accommodate a large number of people in the countryside without destroying it in the process. The Unité d'Habitation Marseille is a communal dwelling still viable even now. As to today's imperatives, the primary directive is to live closer together so as to minimize movement and conserve energy.

Maybe it's too discursive or speculative, particularly in relation to the ubiquity of high-speed informational exchanges, but I think this question of the society—the social—what is left of the capacity of the human species for acting collectively is of relevance to the future of the species, which is very precarious in many ways. If one were to persist with the culture of architecture, and the built environment, and with the potential to provide for social and symbolic space, then the argument about relevance has to begin there. It has to be assumed axiomatically that architecture still has bearing and import, otherwise you can't even begin.

Acknowledgments

This book is by necessity a hybrid project. Part retroactive manifesto, part extended conversation and, perhaps, most importantly, a prologue to future action. It reflects the contributions of multiple protagonists over a sustained period of time. Clients, colleagues, experts, students, and friends have influenced the trajectory of our research and work and have helped us frame many of the ideas that are at the heart of this book. For us, design is a form of research. In the sense that design is iterative, each project is a creative hypothesis that is tested, is given measure, and extends the foundation for future work.

This book was initiated as a series of research studios, first at the University of Pennsylvania School of Design and more recently at the Harvard Graduate School of Design. We are grateful for the support of Dean Marilyn Jordan Taylor at the University of Pennsylvania for the grant that helped make this book possible. We thank Dean Taylor and Chair of Architecture Winka Dubbeldam, whom have both championed an elastic view of the territory of architecture and urbanism at Penn Design. At the GSD, we are indebted to Dean Mohsen Mostafavi, former Chair of Architecture Preston Scott Cohen, and Chair of the Department of Urban Planning and Design Rahul Mehrotra. Their collective leadership has brought a renewed attention to the imperatives of urban research, disciplinary integration, and expanded forums for design exploration.

In particular, we are very grateful to the critics who participated in reviews and contributed to framing the *Terms and Conditions* dialogue: Preston Scott Cohen, Felipe Correa, Keller Easterling, Paul Lewis, Hashim Sarkis, and Nader Tehrani. Professor Kenneth Frampton, whose work continues to inspire, was central to our roundtable discussion, providing an opportunity to reflect on the history of the subject of megaform as well as its future.

The projects here reflect the collective talents and commitment of members of our studio whom always expand the boundaries of what we do. We are deeply grateful to project leaders who have helped bring the work in this book to reality: Patrick Armacost, Clifton Balch, Christopher Ballentine, Mike Harshman, and Todd Hoehn, and Armando Petruccelli. We are also grateful to key team members of our office whom have all given shape to these projects: Michael Blasberg, Mateo Antonio de Cárdenas, Joe Chase, Paúl Duston-Muñoz, Matthew Ferraro, Kian Goh, Hamilton Hadden, Pierre Hoppenot, Bryan Kelley, Hanul Kim, Ina Ko, Justin Kwok, Noah Levy, Lee Lim, Johnny Lin, Joseph Littrell, David Maple, Heather McArthur, Kim Nun, Hugo de Pablo, Evalynn Rosado, Andrew Ruggles, Seungwon Song,

Michael Steiner, Yehre Suh, Joe Vessell, and Darius Woo.

We are indebted to our clients that believed in our work at critical moments and whose leadership helped realize these projects: Kate Bicknell, Frederick Bland, Elizabeth Boylan, Caroline Cunningham, Mike Dausch, Gilbert Delgado, Randy Dias, Teresa Durkin, Lisa Gamsu, Mimi Gardner Gates, MaryAnne Gilmartin, Christopher Glaisek, Eduardo Glandt, Laura Gray, Leonard Greco, Amy Gutmann, David Hollenberg, Dan Huttenlocher, Chris Kern, Jennifer Klein, Bill Lacy, Patrick Lobdell, Greg Lowe, Scot Medbury, Anne Papageorge, Michael Rem, Chris Rogers, Bob Sanna, Judith Shapiro, Jon and Mary Shirley, Debora Spar, the Taekwondo Foundation, Jennifer Wetzel, Ira Winston, and Andrew Winters.

In particular, we are very grateful to the individuals who have informed the evolution of our work. David Leatherbarrow, through his writings and conversations, has articulated and expanded the terrain of our considerations. Mohsen Mostafavi and the late Detlef Mertins have compelled us to focus and refine our ideas and have extended our ongoing dialogue in their writings. At the Museum of Modern Art, Barry Bergdoll, Peter Reed, and Pedro Gadanho, whose writings and curatorial efforts have redefined the nexus of landscape and architecture, have supported and nourished our work. David van der Leer, while at the Guggenheim, offered a public forum through which to present our preliminary research. And the inspiration of our late professors, Colin Rowe and James Stirling, still sustain us.

The intersection of art and architecture has been fertile ground for us. Richard Serra has been an inspiration to work with, and artists Iwan Baan, Mark Dion, Teresita Fernández, Jeff Goldberg, Geoffrey James, Roy McMakin, Thomas Roma, Shuli Sadé, Mark di Suvero, Albert Večerka, and Paul Warchol have taught us new ways to see the reciprocity between art and architecture.

We would also like to thank critically important colleagues and advisors, who in both subtle and profound ways have helped shape our practice: Donald Albrecht, Stan Allen, Thomas Balsley, Barry Bergdoll, Aaron Betsky, Michael Bierut, Hallie Boyce, Joan Busquets, James Corner, Lisa Corrin, Michael DeCandia, Hal Foster, Kenneth Frampton, Eva Franch i Gilabert, Ray Gastil, Rosalie Genevro, Skip Graffam, Bob Heintges, Craig Hodgetts, Casey Jones, Rachel Judlowe, Stephen Kieran, Kent Kleinman, Reed Kroloff, Elizabeth Kubany, Anuradha Mathur, Thom Mayne, Elizabeth Meyer, Laurie Olin, Cesar Pelli, James Polshek, Philippa Polskin, Ali Rahim, Peter Reed, Anne Rieselbach, Terence Riley, Mark Robbins, Raymund Ryan, Zoë Ryan, Robert Stern, and

Charles Waldheim. We owe special thanks to Andrea Leers, friend and mentor, who has provided sustained guidance, and to Romaldo Giurgola, who taught us the value of architecture of consequence.

Bringing a book project to reality requires clarity, diligence, and patience. Justin Fowler's critical voice throughout this process gave identity and direction to the material. His editorial efforts have shaped the texts and helped frame the arguments.

We are grateful to the editors at Princeton Architectural Press, Jennifer Lippert and Meredith Baber, whom have guided and supported the direction for this book. The book was given graphic clarity and visual context through the creative efforts of Adam Michaels and Anna Rieger of Project Projects.

Special thanks go to Kerry O'Connor, whose initial efforts helped lay out the foundation for this book, and to Kao Onishi and Barbara Wilson for their diligence in continuing these efforts.

Finally, we would like to offer a special thanks to Allison Wicks, whose leadership and guidance have been indispensable, and whose grace and intelligence have helped steer this unwieldy project toward completion.

Michael A. Manfredi and Marion Weiss

Authors

Weiss/Manfredi is a multidisciplinary design firm in New York known for its dynamic integration of architecture, art, infrastructure, and landscape design. Weiss/Manfredi has been recognized with the American Academy of Arts and Letters Architecture Award, the Architectural League Emerging Voices Award, New York AIA's Gold Medal, and Harvard University's International Veronica Rudge Green Prize in Urban Design. Both Marion Weiss and Michael A. Manfredi have been inducted into the National Academy, and their work has been exhibited at the Venice Biennale, the Museum of Modern Art, the Cooper-Hewitt, Smithsonian Design Museum, the Guggenheim Museum, and the Louvre.

Marion Weiss is the Graham Chair Professor of Architecture at the University of Pennsylvania's School of Design and has also taught at Harvard, Yale, and Cornell Universities. She is a founding partner of Weiss/Manfredi.

Michael A. Manfredi was the Gensler Visiting Professor of Architecture at Cornell University and has taught at Harvard, Yale, and Princeton Universities, the University of Pennsylvania, and the Institute for Architecture and Urban Studies. He is a founding partner of Weiss/Manfredi.

Contributors

Barry Bergdoll is the Meyer Schapiro Professor of Art History and Archaeology at Columbia University and curator in the Department of Architecture and Design at the Museum of Modern Art.

Preston Scott Cohen is the Gerald M. McCue Professor and former chair of architecture at Harvard University Graduate School of Design and principal of Preston Scott Cohen, Inc., in Cambridge, Massachusetts. He is the author of *Contested Symmetries*, and coauthor with Erika Naginski of *The Return of Nature* and *Lightfall*.

Felipe Correa is an associate professor and director of the urban design degree program at the Harvard University Graduate School of Design. He is the cofounder of Somatic Collaborative, a research-based design practice, and the South America Project, a transcontinental applied research network.

Keller Easterling is an architect, urbanist, and writer. She is professor of architecture at Yale University School of Architecture.

Justin Fowler received his MArch from the Harvard University Graduate School of Design and is currently a PhD candidate at the Princeton University School of Architecture. He is a founding editor of *Manifest: A Journal of American Architecture and Urbanism* and his writing has appeared in magazines such as *Volume*, *PIN-UP*, *Thresholds*, *Topos*, and *Domus*.

Kenneth Frampton is the Ware Professor of Architecture at Columbia University Graduate School of Architecture, Planning, and Preservation. A historian and critic of architecture, he is the author of numerous books including *Modern Architecture: A Critical History*; *Studies in Tectonic Culture, Labor, Work, and Architecture*; and the forthcoming *A Genealogy of Modern Architecture: Comparative Critical Analysis of Built Form*.

Paul Lewis is founding partner of LTL Architects, located in New York City. He is an associate professor at the Princeton University School of Architecture.

Hashim Sarkis is an architect practicing in Cambridge, Massachusetts, and Beirut. He is the dean of the School of Architecture and Planning at MIT.

Nader Tehrani is a professor of architecture at MIT, where he served as head of the department from 2010 to 2014. He is also principal of NADAAA, a multidisciplinary practice with projects in urbanism, architecture, and fabrication.

Notes

Terms and Conditions

1   *Josep Lluís Sert: The Architect of Urban Design, 1953–1969*, ed. Eric Mumford, Hashim Sarkis, and Neyran Turan (New Haven, CT: Yale University Press, 2008), 209–10.
2   *Landform Building: Architecture's New Terrain*, ed. Stan Allen and Marc McQuade (Princeton, NJ: Princeton University School of Architecture, 2011), 262.
3   *The New City: Architecture and Urban Renewal*, Museum of Modern Art (New York: Museum of Modern Art, 1967), 22.
4   Reyner Banham, *Megastructure: Urban Futures of the Recent Past* (New York: Harper and Row, 1976), 29.
5   Vincent Scully Jr., *American Architecture and Urbanism* (New York: Holt, Rinehart and Winston, 1969), 154.
6   Sigfried Giedion, *Space, Time and Architecture: The Growth of a New Tradition* (Cambridge, MA: Harvard University Press, 1967), 862.
7   Foreign Office Architects, *Phylogenesis: FOA's Ark* (Barcelona: Actar, 2003), 232.
8   Banham, *Megastructure*, 13.
9   Ibid.
10 Le Corbusier, *The City of To-morrow and Its Planning* (Cambridge, MA: MIT Press, 1971), 270.
11 Banham, *Megastructure*, 217.
12 Kenneth Frampton, "Megaform as Urban Landscape" (Urbana: University of Illinois at Urbana-Champaign, 2010), 11.
13 Banham, *Megastructure*, 55.
14 Jürgen Joedicke, introduction to *Candilis Josic Woods: Building for People*, by Shadrach Woods (New York: Praeger Publishers, 1968), 9.
15 Frampton, "Megaform as Urban Landscape," 46.
16 Colin Rowe and Fred Koetter, *Collage City* (Cambridge, MA: MIT Press, 1984), 48.
17 Banham, *Megastructure*, 54.
18 Le Corbusier, *The City of To-morrow and Its Planning*, 301.
19 Scully, *American Architecture and Urbanism*, 100.
20 Banham, *Megastructure*, 32.
21 Edgar Chambless, *Roadtown* (New York: Roadtown Press, 1910), 35–36.
22 Banham, *Megastructure*, 218.
23 Alison Smithson and Peter Smithson, *The Charged Void: Urbanism*, ed. Chuihua Judy Chung (New York: Monacelli Press, 2005), 56.

Social Infrastructures

1   Allen, *Landform Building*, 238–41.
2   Jonah Lehrer, "Groupthink," New Yorker, January 30, 2012, 25.

Megaform and Public Natures

1   Banham, *Megastructure*, 30.
2   Robert Somol, "Green Dots 101," *Hunch* 11 (2007): 34.

Project Credits

Olympic Sculpture Park
Client: Seattle Art Museum

Weiss/Manfredi Team (Architecture, Landscape, and Site Design)
Design Partners: Marion Weiss and Michael A. Manfredi
Project Manager: Christopher Ballentine
Project Architects: Todd Hoehn and Yehre Suh
Project Team: Patrick Armacost, Michael Blasberg, Emily Clanahan, Beatrice Eleazar, Hamilton Hadden, Mike Harshman, Mustapha Jundi, John Peek, and Akari Takebayashi
Additional Team Members: Lauren Crahan, Kian Goh, Justin Kwok, and Lee Lim

Consultant Team
Structural and Civil Engineering Consultant: Magnusson Klemencic Associates
Landscape Architecture Consultant: Charles Anderson Landscape Architecture
Mechanical and Electrical Engineering Consultant: ABACUS Engineered Systems
Lighting Design Consultant: Brandston Partnership Inc.
Geotechnical Engineering Consultant: Hart Crowser
Environmental Consultant: Aspect Consulting
Aquatic Engineering Consultant: Anchor QEA, LLC
Graphics Consultant: Pentagram
Security, Audiovisual, and Information Technology Consultant: Arup
Catering and Food Service Consultant: Bon Appetit
Kitchen Consultant: JLR Design
Retail Consultant: Doyle + Associates
Architectural Site Representation: Owens Richards Architects, PLLC
Project Management: Barrientos LLC
General Contractor: Sellen Construction

Toronto Lower Don Lands
Client: Toronto Waterfront Revitalization Corporation, City of Toronto

Weiss/Manfredi Team
Design Partners: Marion Weiss and Michael A. Manfredi
Project Architect: Todd Hoehn
Project Team: Patrick Armacost, Cheryl Baxter, Beatrice Eleazar, Hamilton Hadden, Justin Kwok, Lee Lim, Sun Na, and Yehre Suh

Consultant Team
Landscape Architecture Consultant: DTAH
Structural Engineering Consultant: Weidlinger Associates, Inc.
Traffic, Structural, and Civil Engineering Consultant: McCormick Rankin Corporation

Ecology Restoration and Regenerative Design Consultant: Biohabitats Inc.
Hydrology, Geotechnical, and Shoreline Engineering Consultant: Golder Associates Ltd.

Hunter's Point South Waterfront Park
Client: New York City Economic Development Corporation, Office of the Deputy Mayor for Economic Development, NYC Department of Parks and Recreation
Park Designers: Thomas Balsley Associates / Weiss/Manfredi
Prime Consultant and Infrastructure Designer: Arup

Weiss/Manfredi Team
Design Partners: Marion Weiss and Michael A. Manfredi
Project Manager: Christopher Ballentine
Project Architects: Lee Lim and Michael Steiner
Project Team: Michael Blasberg and Hyoung-Gul Kook
Additional Team Members: Alice Chai, Nick Elliot, and Joe Vessell
Thomas Balsley Associates Team
Design Principal: Thomas Balsley
Project Team: John Donnelly, Christian Gabriel, Michael Koontz, and Dale Schafer

Consultant Team
Civil Engineering, Structural Engineering, and Lighting Design Consultant: Arup
Mechanical, Electrical, and Plumbing Engineering Consultant: A. G. Consulting Engineering, PC
Geotechnical Engineering Consultant: Yu & Associates, Inc.
Shoreline Engineering Consultant: Halcrow
Cost Estimating Consultant: VJ Associates
Construction Manager: The Liro Group
General Contractor: Galvin Brothers Construction Company

Taekwondo Park
Client: Taekwondo Promotion Foundation

Weiss/Manfredi Team
Design Partners: Marion Weiss and Michael A. Manfredi
Project Managers: Rhett Russo and Yehre Suh
Project Team: Patrick Armacost, Todd Hoehn, Justin Kwok, Lee Lim, Joseph Littrell, Armando Petruccelli, Andrew Ruggles, Austin Tragni, Joseph Vessell, and Yoonsun Yang
Additional Team Members: Cheryl Baxter, Alice Chai, Beth Eckels, Jocelyn Froimovich, Hamilton Hadden, Huei Ming Juang, Justin Kwok, Kim Nun, Lindsey Sherman, and Michael Steiner

Consultant Team
Taekwondo Specialty Consultants: Master Sung

Chul Wang and Master Jun Chul Wang
Architect's Local Representative: Dongwoo Architects Co., Ltd.

Brooklyn Botanic Garden Visitor Center
Client: Brooklyn Botanic Garden

Weiss/Manfredi Team (Architecture, Landscape, and Site Design)
Design Partners: Marion Weiss and Michael A. Manfredi
Project Manager: Armando Petruccelli
Project Architects: Hamilton Hadden, Justin Kwok, and Michael Steiner
Project Team: Christopher Ballentine, Cheryl Baxter, Michael Blasberg, and Paúl Duston-Muñoz
Additional Team Members: Jeremy Babel, Caroline Emerson, Eleonora Flammina, Aaron Hollis, Jonathan Schwartz, and Yoonsun Yang
Additional Competition Team Members: Patrick Armacost, Kian Goh, and Mike Harshman

Consultant Team
Structural and Civil Engineering Consultant: Weidlinger Associates, Inc.
Mechanical, Electrical, Plumbing, Fire Protection, and Information Technology Engineering Consultant: Jaros, Baum & Bolles
Geothermal and Geotechnical Engineering Consultant: Langan Engineering and Environmental Services
Landscape Architecture Consultant: HM White Site Architects
Lighting Design Consultant: Brandston Partnership Inc.
Cost Estimating Consultant: AMIS Inc.
Environmental Consultant: Vidaris, Inc.
Retail Consultant: Jeanne Giordano Ltd.
Audiovisual, Acoustics, and Security Consultant: Cerami & Associates, Inc.
Security Consultant: TM Technology Partners, Inc.
Food Service Consultant: Ricca Newmark Design
Curtain Wall Consultant: R. A. Heintges & Associates
Code Consultant: Code Consultants, Inc.
Traffic Consultant: Sam Schwartz Engineering
Construction Manager: The Liro Group
General Contractor: E. W. Howell

Barnard College Diana Center
Client: Barnard College

Weiss/Manfredi Team
Design Partners: Marion Weiss and Michael A. Manfredi
Project Manager: Mike Harshman
Project Architects: Clifton Balch, Kian Goh, Kim Nun, and Yehre Suh
Project Team: Patrick Armacost, Michael Blasberg, Beth Eckels, Hamilton Hadden,

Patrick Hazari, Todd Hoehn, Bryan Kelley, Justin Kwok, Lee Lim, Nick Shipes, Michael Steiner, and Tae-Young Yoon
Additional Team Members: Anastasia Kostrominova and Jason Ro

Consultant Team
Mechanical, Electrical, Plumbing, Fire Protection, and Vertical Transportation Engineering Consultant: Jaros, Baum & Bolles
Structural Engineering Consultant: Severud Associates
Civil Engineering Consultant: Langan Engineering and Environmental Services
Curtain Wall Consultant: R. A. Heintges & Associates
Lighting Design Consultant: Brandston Partnership Inc.
Landscape Architecture Consultant: HM White Site Architects
Audiovisual, Information Technology, General Acoustics, and Security Consultant: Cerami & Associates, Inc., with T. M. Technology Partners, Inc.
Food Service Consultant: Ricca Newmark Design
Retail Consultant: Jeanne Giordano
Cost Estimating Consultant: AMIS Inc.
Sustainability Consultant: Vidaris, Inc.
Theatre Consultant: Fisher Dachs Associates
Theatre Acoustics Consultant: Jaffe Holden Acoustics, Inc.
Waterproofing Consultant: James R. Gainfort, AIA, Consulting Architects, PC
Construction Manager: Bovis Lend Lease

Sylvan Theater at the Washington Monument
Client: Trust for the National Mall
Lead Designers: Weiss/Manfredi + Olin

Weiss/Manfredi Team
Design Partners: Marion Weiss and Michael A. Manfredi
Project Manager: Mike Harshman
Competition Team Leaders: Bryan Kelley, Noah Z. Levy, and Allison Wicks
Additional Team Members: Patrick Armacost, Constantine Bouras, Justin Kwok, Joe Littrell, Kerry O'Connor, Andrew Ruggles, Joe Vessell, and Tsvetelina Zdraveva
Project Team: Bryan Kelley and Hugo de Pablo

Olin Team
Design Partners: Hallie Boyce and Skip Graffam
Competition Team Leader: Greg Burrell
Competition Team: Jennifer Birkeland, Chris Landau, Vivian Martinez, Nick Mitchell, Henry Moll, Ben Monette, Laura Rennekamp, Jenn Richey-Nicholas, and Danni Sinisi
Project Manager: Leigh Ann Campbell
Green Infrastructure Partner: Stephen Benz
Project Team: Ari Miller and Dana Williamson

Consultant Team
Structural and Civil Engineering Consultant: Magnusson Klemencic Associates
Performance Planning Consultant: Fisher Dachs Associates
Mechanical Engineering Consultant: Jaros Baum & Bolles
Acoustics Consultant: Threshold Acoustics LLC
Sustainability Consultant: Atelier Ten
Performance Art Advocate: Sphinx Organization
Circulation and Planning Consultant: Space Syntax
History and Archaeology Consultant: John Milner Associates, Inc.
Economics Consultant: HR&A Advisors
Lighting Design Consultant: Fisher Marantz Stone
Artist: Studio Echelman
Maintenance and Operations Consultant: ETM Associates, LLC
Signage and Wayfinding Consultant: Bruce Mau Design
Ecology Consultant: Habitat by Design
Transportation Consultant: Gorove/Slade Associates, Inc.
Security Consultant: Ducibella Venter & Santore
Food Service Consultant: James N. Davella Consulting, LLC
Community Outreach Consultant: Milton Puryear
Irrigation Designer: Lynch & Associates
Surveyor: Wiles Mensch Corporation
Geotechnical Engineering Consultant: GeoConcepts Engineering, Inc.
Blast Consultant: Hinman Consulting Engineers, Inc.
Code Consultant: Code Consultants, Inc.
Cost Estimating Consultant: Davis Langdon (AECOM)

Novartis Visitor Reception
Client: Novartis Pharmaceuticals Corporation

Weiss/Manfredi Team (Architecture, Landscape, and Site Design)
Design Partners: Marion Weiss and Michael A. Manfredi
Project Manager: Christopher Ballentine
Project Architects: Matthew Ferraro and Justin Kwok
Project Team: Johnny Lin and Andrew Ruggles
Additional Team Members: Clifton Balch, Michael Blasberg, Todd Hoehn, Hyoung-Gul Kook, and Lee Lim

Consultant Team
Structural Engineering Consultant: Severud Associates
Mechanical, Electrical, Plumbing, Fire Protection, and Security Consultant: Cosentini Associates
Curtain Wall Consultant: R. A. Heintges & Associates

Renewable Energy Consultant: RELAB, LLC
Lighting Design Consultant: Brandston Partnership Inc.
Cost Estimating Consultant: Davis Langdon (AECOM)
Code Consultant: Code Consultants, Inc.
Waterproofing Consultant: James R. Gainfort, AIA Consulting Architects, PC
Construction Manager: Sordoni Construction Company

Novartis Office Building
Client: Novartis Pharmaceuticals Corporation

Weiss/Manfredi Team
Design Partners: Marion Weiss and Michael A. Manfredi
Project Manager: Clifton Balch
Project Architects: Joseph Chase and Matthew Ferraro
Project Team: Joseph Vessell
Additional Team Members: Cheryl Baxter, Michael Blasberg, Carol Chang, Mateo Antonio de Cárdenas, Hanul Kim, Noah Z. Levy, Armando Petruccelli, and Asami Takahashi

Consultant Team
Structural Engineering Consultant: Severud Associates
Mechanical, Electrical, Plumbing, Fire Protection, and Security Consultant: Cosentini Associates
Curtain Wall Consultant: R. A. Heintges & Associates
Lighting Design Consultant: Brandston Partnership, Inc.
Food Service Consultant: James N. Davella Consulting, LLC
Audiovisual and Acoustics Consultant: Shen Milsom & Wilke
Elevator Consultant: Van Deusen & Associates
Cost Estimating Consultant: Davis Langdon (AECOM)
Code Consultant: Code Consultants, Inc.
Waterproofing Consultant: James R. Gainfort, AIA Consulting Architects, PC
Construction Manager: Turner Construction Company

Cornell NYC Tech
Co-Location Building
Client: Forest City Ratner Companies

Weiss/Manfredi Team
Design Partners: Marion Weiss and Michael A. Manfredi
Project Manager: Mike Harshman
Project Architects: Pierre Hoppenot, Heather McArthur, and Joe Vessell
Project Team: Hanul Kim
Additional Team Members: James Murray, Kerry O'Connor, and Erin Saven

Competition Team: Joe Chase, Todd Hoehn,
Jina Kim, Lee Lim, Joe Vessell, and
Allison Wicks

Consultant Team
Structural Engineering Consultant: Thornton
Tomasetti, Inc.
Mechanical, Electrical, Plumbing, and Fire
Protection Engineering Consultant: Jaros,
Baum & Bolles
Curtain Wall Consultant: R. A. Heintges &
Associates
Lighting Design Consultant: Renfro Design
Group
Code Consultant: Code Consultants, Inc.
Audiovisual and Acoustics Consultant: Arup

Krishna P. Singh Center for Nanotechnology
Client: University of Pennsylvania

*Weiss/Manfredi Team (Architecture, Landscape,
and Site Design)*
Design Partners: Marion Weiss and
Michael A. Manfredi
Project Manager: Todd Hoehn
Senior Project Architect: Mike Harshman
Project Architects: Ina Ko and Kim Nun
Project Team: Bryan Kelley and Michael Steiner
Additional Team Members: Patrick Armacost,
Cheryl Baxter, Michael Blasberg, Beth Eckels,
Jocelyn Froimovich, Patrick Hazari, Jina Kim,
Justin Kwok, Andrew Ruggles, Joe Vessell, and
Joe Vidich

Consultant Team
Lab, Mechanical, Electrical, Plumbing, and Fire
Protection Engineering Consultant: M+W
Group
Structural Engineering Consultant:
Severud Associates
Civil Engineering Consultant: Stantec
Sustainability Consultant: Vidaris, Inc.
Audiovisual and Acoustics Consultant:
Cerami & Associates, Inc.
Curtain Wall Consultant: R. A. Heintges &
Associates
Elevator Consultant: Van Deusen & Associates
Food Service Consultant: James N. Davella
Consulting, LLC
Lighting Design Consultant: Brandston
Partnership Inc.
Green Roof Consultant: Roofmeadow
Electromagnetic Interference Consultant:
VitaTech
Vibration Isolation Consultant: Colin Gordon
Associates
Cost Estimating Consultant: Davis Langdon
(AECOM)
Construction Manager: Gilbane

Image Credits
Images are by Weiss/Manfredi unless
otherwise noted.

Evolutionary Infrastructures
© Iwan Baan: 16, 18–19, 32, 35, 46 (bottom), 57
(top, bottom), 58 (bottom), 62–63
© Ben Benschneider: 22, 23, 28–29, 37 (top,
middle), 44–45, 46 (top), 48, 54–55
© 2014 Calder Foundation, New York / Artists
Rights Society (ARS), New York: 16, 35
Michael Dickter / MKA: 41 (top)
© Fondation Le Corbusier (F.L.C.) / ADAGP,
Paris / Artist Rights Society (ARS), New York
2014: 11
© Bruce Moore: 40 (top)
© Lara Swimmer: 26–27
Taekwondo Promotion Foundation: 112–13
Taekwondo Promotion Foundation, photo collage
by Weiss/Manfredi: 121
Thomas Balsley Associates / Weiss/Manfredi: 85,
88–89, 90–91 (top), 93 (top), 95, 108 (top)
Toronto and Regional Conservation Authority
Archives: 66
University of Washington Libraries Special
Collections: 20 (left)
© Albert Večerka / Esto: Front and back cover,
80–81, 83, 94–95, 98–99, 101, 102, 106–7, 108
(bottom), 109, 130–31, 133–35, 138, 140–41, 143,
144, 146–48, 150–51, 152 (top), 153–56, 158–59
© Robert Wade: 50–51
© Paul Warchol: 37 (bottom), 43, 52, 53, 56, 59
© Wade Zimmerman: 104–5, 110–11

Terms and Conditions
© Archigram Archives 2013: 172
© Iwan Baan: 184
Courtesy of Preston Scott Cohen: 206 (left)
Ceri Edmunds: 171 (bottom)
© Hugh Ferriss: 193
© F.L.C. / ADAGP, Paris / Artist Rights Society
(ARS), New York 2014: 183
Courtesy of Foreign Office Architects: 174
(bottom left, bottom right)
© Raymond Hood: 202 (left)
© Timothy Hursley: 180 (bottom)
Joumana Jamhouri, courtesy of Hashim Sarkis
Studios: 208 (right)
© Akio Kawasumi, courtesy of Tange Associates:
160
Alexandria Lee: 178, 201 (top left, bottom)
Library of Congress Prints and Photographs
Division: 206 (right)
Library of Congress Prints and Photographs
Division, Paul Rudolph Archive: 182
Courtesy of LTL Architects: 191
Courtesy of Maki and Associates: 176 (bottom)
National Park Service Olmsted Archives, Boston
Parks Department and Olmsted Architects:
177
Courtesy of OMA: 173, 186
Miriam Roure Parera: 209

Public Domain: 165, 169, 180 (top), 196, 202
(right)
Pablo Roquero: 174 (top)
Matt Scarlett: 201 (top right)
Micah Sittig: 188
Courtesy of Nader Tehrani: 176 (top)
© The Museum of Modern Art / Licensed by
SCALA / Art Resource, NY / © 2014 Artist
Rights Society (ARS), New York / VG Bild-
Kunst, Bonn: 205
Marc Veraart, https://www.flickr.com/photos/
marcveraart/: 171 (top)
Sung Ming Whang: 192
Marcin Wichary: 199
Candilis-Josic-Woods: 181
Jean Yasmine, courtesy of Hashim Sarkis Studios:
208 (left)

Social Infrastructures
AC Photo: 322 (bottom)
Sarah Blitzer: 219 (right)
Carol M. Highsmith's America, Library of
Congress, Prints and Photographs Division:
258 (left)
Kilograph: 314–15
Courtesy of Maki and Associates: 217
Jim Pruitt: 256–57
Public Domain: 219 (left), 258 (right)
Alexander Torrenegra, http://www.flickr.com/
photos/alextorrenegra/3215957700/, CC-BY
2.0: 222
© Albert Večerka / Esto: 224, 229, 230, 232–33,
235, 239, 245–47, 249–51, 254–55, 274–75, 277,
280–81, 284–85, 316–17, 319, 325, 327, 328 (top
left, bottom left), 329–34, 336–39, 341, 344–47,
348 (top), 350–51
View of the University of Virginia, Albert and
Shirley Small Special Collections Library,
University of Virginia: 215
© Paul Warchol: 236–38, 242–43 (top), 253,
282–83, 288–89, 291–93, 295 (bottom), 297, 298
(bottom), 299–301
Weiss/Manfredi and Olin: 259, 260, 263, 264–65
(bottom), 266–67, 270–73

Megaform and Public Natures
© Iwan Baan: 360, 371
© F.L.C. / ADAGP, Paris / Artist Rights Society
(ARS), New York 2014: 369 (right)
Ana María León: 359 (left)
L'Illa Diagonal, https://www.flickr.com/photos/
lilladiagonal/3635554852/, CC-BY-NC-ND
2.0: 359 (right)
Courtesy of Office of Kevin Roche, John Dinkeloo
and Associates LLC: 369 (left)
The Port Authority of New York and New Jersey:
352
Flickr user: wadester16, https://www.flickr.
com/photos/36071029@N05/3537560291/,
CC-BY-SA 2.0: 365